COLORADO'S DINOSAURS

By John T. Jenkins, Jr. and Jannice L. Jenkins

Pen and ink and charcoal drawings by Donna Braginetz
Maps drawn by Larry Scott and Ty Ortiz
Book design by Rick Ciminelli, State Design Center

Colorado Geological Survey
Division of Minerals and Geology
Department of Natural Resources
Denver, Colorado
1993

A skeletal reconstruction of
Stegosaurus, Colorado's State Fossil

Figure Credits

These figures are © copyrighted, all rights reserved: Cover Illustration, title page illustration, 1–4, 10, 12–19, 22–29, 30c, 31–39, 41–45, 47–50, 52–63, 66–73, 75, 76, 79, 82–84—Dino Productions; 5, 74, 78—Denver Museum of Natural History; 8, 9, 11—Field Museum of Natural History; 30a, 30b, 46—Dr. Robert Young; 51—Dr. Martin Lockley, University of Colorado at Denver; 64 (by Harley Armstrong), 65 (by Gretal Daugherty), 80 (by Jerry Van Wyngarden), 81 (by Al Ligrani)—Museum of Western Colorado.

These figures produced by state agencies are in the public domain: 7, 77—Colorado Department of Highways; 6—Colorado School of Mines Geology Museum; 20 (modified from A. E. Sanborn), 21, 40—Colorado Geological Survey.

Colorado Geological Survey,
Denver, CO 80203
Division of Minerals and Geology
Department of Natural Resources
State of Colorado
1993

ISBN 1-884216-47-1

Contents

page

FIGURES

ACKNOWLEDGEMENTS

We wish to thank Dr. Martin Lockley, Paleontology Professor at the University of Colorado at Denver; Dr. Robert Young, consulting geologist, Grand Junction; Dr. Richard Stucky, Paleontologist, Denver Museum of Natural History; and Dan Chure, Chief Paleontologist, Dinosaur National Monument for reviewing the manuscript and offering their constructive comments.

We also express our appreciation to the following institutions, groups, and individuals: Denver Museum of Natural History—Harvey Markman, Curator of Geology; Garden Park Paleontological Society; University of Colorado at Boulder—Dr. Robert Bakker; Brigham Young University—Dr. Wade Miller and Ken Stadtman; Museum of Western Colorado in Grand Junction; Dinosaur National Monument; San Diego State University—Dr. David Archibald.

Special thanks go to the Friends of Dinosaur Ridge for their financial contribution in tribute to the memory of John Jenkins. John Rold, former Director of the Colorado Geological Survey, deserves our appreciation for his effort in getting the story of Colorado's dinosaurs published.

SLEUTHING THE PAST

Alone Native American hunter stops in his tracks a little less than 10,000 years ago. The early spring weather is cold and windy, yet he pauses to examine some bones lying on the ground along what will later be known as part of the Dakota Hogback and still later as Dinosaur Ridge. He stands just north of a site that in a few thousand years will become the town of Morrison, Colorado. The size of the bones reminds the hunter of the large mammoths (Figure 1) which he and his tribe used to

hunt but have not seen for several seasons. As he examines the remains his mind fills with questions. He wonders what sort of animal these bones belong to and how long ago it died. Unlike the bones of recently dead animals, these bones are larger, darker in color and are as heavy as the rocks lying around them. Many are broken and appear to have lain on the surface for a long time. Some are even imbedded in the surrounding rocks.

The empty howl of the wind reminds him of the emptiness in his stomach so, for today, there will be no answer to his questions. He hastens on with his hunt for a living creature. He only hopes that his chance find of the remains of such a gigantic creature will bring him luck on his hunt. In the thousands of years since this chance discovery the relentless forces of erosion will continue to wear down the ridge, weathering more bones and turning them to dust as they are exposed.

In 1877 another explorer is on the ridge north of Morrison. This new investigator is a teacher and a hunter of fossils in his spare time. He has journeyed southeast from his

home in Golden, Colorado to explore a ridge of rocks. His keen eyes are searching for those often incomplete, yet tantalizing, bits of evidence which indicate what life was like before man came upon the scene. He has no idea he will be rewarded with a totally unexpected discovery of fossilized dinosaur bones. At almost the same time 100 miles to the south, another amateur paleontologist (a geologist who specializes in the study of the history of life on earth), who also happens to be a teacher, is making a similar discovery in an area called Garden Park north of the town of Canon City, Colorado. Their two discoveries will soon catapult Colorado to national recognition as *the* place to go to collect dinosaur fossils.

In the ensuing years these sites will prove to be only the first of many which have helped Colorado gain its status as a major source of dinosaur fossils. Today, unique discoveries in the western states of Wyoming, Utah, Montana, New Mexico, Arizona, and South and North Dakota, have expanded the collecting sites to include almost every state in the American west. All of these states together have yielded literally hundreds of tons of dinosaur bones. Many of these discoveries

Figure 1. A wooly mammoth, one of the many large Pleistocene or Ice Age mammals, which lived in Colorado over 10,000 years ago.

are on display in museums from coast to coast in the United States.

Besides having great historical significance, Colorado is still in the limelight today as new or more complete dinosaur fossils are discovered. As in the early days of research, amateur and professional paleontologists continue to work side by side in unraveling the mystery of dinosaur fossils found in the rocks. In the past, most specimens were collected for exhibition, description and/or preservation. This procedure continues today with today's researchers still trying to find definitive answers to questions posed years ago by scientists as they gazed upon dinosaur bones.

Many of today's scientists who study dinosaurs are geologists who specialize in studying ancient life. Although there have been great advances in the science of geology since 1877, geologists are still in search of answers to many earlier questions about dinosaurs. These include: What kind of animals were dinosaurs? How did dinosaurs live? Why did they become extinct? What other animals lived at the same time as dinosaurs? What was the climate like when dinosaurs lived? In order to answer these questions, geologists look for small as well as large fossils, including bones, eggs, tracks and fossilized plants, they make measure-

Figure 2. These dinosaur bones are in rocks deposited over 140-million years ago during the Age of Reptiles. Both the bones and the sand were once part of the sediment being carried along by an ancient river.

ments and maps showing how bones, or perhaps tracks, may be arranged at a site, and they gather information about ancient environments by studying the rocks which entomb the bones (Figure 2).

There is a wealth of geological and paleontological data to be collected at any dinosaur site. Often these data are incomplete, for such is the case of the rock and fossil record. Collecting these data is a slow and meticulous process. As more data become available earlier interpretations about the lives and times of dinosaurs may change. Some of these changes are dramatic and in other cases the concepts remain the same.

Unraveling the mystery of dinosaurs is a dynamic story which continues today. In the past Colorado has figured prominently in this long running mystery. Today, Colorado scientists and their colleagues from around the world conduct research programs related to Colorado's dinosaurs. The following pages chronicle both the rich history and the story which unfolds today. This narrative ends with details on where people can go to either recapture a feel of the historic glory or experience the excitement surrounding current research related to Colorado's dinosaur story.

A RICH HISTORY OF COLLECTING DINOSAUR GIANTS

COLORADO—THE FIRST IN THE WEST

NINETEEN HUNDRED AND NINETY-ONE marked the 150th anniversary of the concept of a "dinosaur" and, yet despite several generations of study, the mystique surrounding dinosaurs still remains. Colorado's dinosaurs still make headlines when a new or perhaps more complete dinosaur fossil is discovered. Many people who have an interest in dinosaurs are intrigued that Colorado often remains in the news. In the past, Colorado held the distinction of being the first state west of the Mississippi River where nearly complete skeletons of large dinosaurs were discovered. For the first time, researchers had enough evidence to develop a more accurate picture of what these extinct animals may have looked like. Four sites figured prominently in the historical collecting of dinosaur fossils in Colorado (Figure 3). Two of these sites are nestled along the Front Range between Denver and Canon City. Two other sites are on Colorado's Western Slope, one near Grand

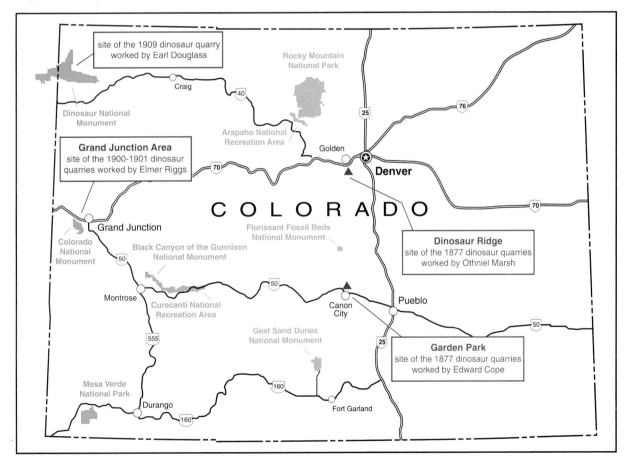

Figure 3. Location map showing the four historical sites which helped establish Colorado as a major source of dinosaur fossils. All four sites have yielded dinosaur fossils that are around 137- to 153-million years old.

Junction and the other being the world renowned Dinosaur National Monument, located west of the towns of Craig and Dinosaur, Colorado at the Utah border. In one form or another all of these historical sites are active today.

As the rush to the dinosaurs of the American West began in the late 1800s, academicians of the day headed west to claim their share of the bounty of dinosaur fossils. Unfortunately, no one west of the Mississippi River was a dinosaur expert so many tons of quarried dinosaur bones from Colorado sites were shipped east in a mad dash to reconstruct the biggest and best dinosaur skeletons for display in museums east of the Mississippi. Although the fossils have in some cases been moved from museum to museum since they were collected, many are still on display in institutions such as the Smithsonian Institution in Washington, D. C., the Field Museum of Natural History in Chicago, Illinois, the Peabody Museum of Natural History in New Haven, Connecticut, the Cleveland Museum of Natural History in Cleveland, Ohio and the Carnegie Museum of Natural History in Pittsburgh, Pennsylvania. In Colorado, dinosaur fossils are on display at the Denver Museum of Natural History in Denver, the University of Colorado Museum, in the Henderson Building on the Boulder campus, the Dinosaur Valley Museum in Grand Junction, the Delta County Museum in Delta, Colorado and Dinosaur National Monument.

HAYDEN'S EXPLORATION OF THE WEST

To develop a feel for the history of dinosaur collecting it is necessary to return to the late 1800s. The United States was in an expansionist mode and geologist Dr. Ferdinand V. Hayden and his crew were in the midst of a ten year study, from 1869 to 1879, documenting the geology and geography of the western United States. While in Colorado they discovered a large fossilized vertebra which they sent to Dr. Joseph Leidy, a noted naturalist of the day, for identification. Dr. Leidy identified the bone as one of the vertebra from the carnivorous dinosaur *Antrodemus.* Today this dinosaur is known as *Allosaurus.* This isolated bone was a harbinger of things to come.

By 1877 Hayden had finished his exploration of Colorado and had published the *Atlas of Colorado.* Early the same year, only one year after Colorado had become a state, two startling discoveries of large quantities of dinosaur bones would catapult Colorado to national fame. Within months of one another, two school teachers and amateur paleontologists made serendipitous discoveries while on separate outings within 100 miles of each other. Neither was looking for dinosaur bones; instead both were on the hunt for plant fossils from the Cretaceous Period (136- to 65-million years ago). They had no idea they would make discoveries that would set the stage for the rush to the dinosaurs of the American West.

GARDEN PARK AND MORRISON QUARRIES

In January of 1877 Ormel W. Lucas, a teacher and amateur paleontologist who resided in Canon City, Colorado, was exploring an area immediately north of town called Garden Park. His search for fossil plants was quickly forgotten when he discovered large dinosaur bones eroding from the red and gray mudstones of what would be later known as the Morrison Formation. An account of Lucas' discovery appeared in the local newspaper the same month, but the magnitude of his discovery was not realized until later that year when his fossilized bones were identified as the remains of *Camarasaurus,* one of the giant sauropods which lived in Colorado over 137-million years ago.

Two months after his startling find Lucas wrote to Edward Drinker Cope, a renowned paleontologist who at the time was Paleontologist and Naturalist at the Philadelphia Academy of Science. Lucas included some fossil dinosaur specimens with his March, 1877 letter to Cope. By the time Cope received the package, his interest in Colorado had been tweaked as he had received some dinosaur fossils that another teacher, Arthur Lakes, had discovered north of Morrison, Colorado. The Morrison area was out of the grasp of Cope for Othniel Charles Marsh, another eminent paleontologist and Cope's arch rival, had laid claim to all discoveries in the Morrison area on behalf of the Yale Peabody Museum. Cope grudgingly returned the specimens which

Figure 4. Location of Marsh's main quarry in Garden Park near Canon City, Colorado. Marsh's crew collected dinosaur bones from the reddish colored rocks immediately above the resistant sandstone ledge that goes from the left to the right in the picture. Unfortunately all of Cope's quarries are overgrown today.

dinosaur bones were of better quality, larger size and more of the skeleton was preserved! Marsh's luck in Garden Park was not as good as it was near Morrison. One of his quarries was vandalized and the other proved to be more difficult to work because the bones were covered by thick overburden and were very difficult to extract from a well cemented sandstone. Figure 4 shows the site of the main Marsh quarry as it looks today. Marsh quarried bones from the top of a resistant sandstone which millions of years ago was deposited by an ancient river.

After three field seasons Garden Park fell quiet until 1915 and 1916 when Dallas (Dall) DeWeese, one of the city fathers of Canon City, a Victorian-style naturalist and a big game hunter, became interested in dinosaurs. His explorations of the Garden Park area were quickly rewarded with the discovery of a partially complete *Diplodocus* skeleton (Figure 5). It was found in same rocks that both Edward Cope and Othniel Marsh excavated in the late 1870s.

Lakes had sent him. When the specimens from Lucas arrived Cope acted quickly and retained Lucas to help with the Garden Park excavation which was only about 100 miles south of Marsh's site.

Throughout the summer of 1877 crews from the Philadelphia Academy of Sciences and the Peabody Museum feverishly labored in quarries at Garden Park and the ridge north of Morrison. They extracted tons of large dinosaur bones which were shipped back to the east coast. Although their primary focus was to collect dinosaur fossils, both crews found fossils of turtles, crocodiles and fish which lived alongside the dinosaurs. Future geological studies would reveal that the rocks and dinosaur fossils in Garden Park and the Morrison area were the same geologic age, Late

Jurassic (156- to 137-million years old). These rocks were later named the Morrison Formation for the town of Morrison which was located near the site where geologists first described the rocks.

Historical accounts of the work near Morrison and at Garden Park indicate that competition was fierce. At one point the Peabody Museum crew opened two quarries near Cope's sites in Garden Park because their spies felt that Cope's

Figure 5. Excavation of the partial skeleton of a *Diplodocus* from the Morrison Formation in Garden Park in 1916 by Dall DeWeese. In the photograph the vertebrae (bones of the backbone) have already been excavated, numbered and are ready for transportation.

DeWeese's subsequent donation of these bones to the Denver Museum of Natural History was instrumental in starting the museum's paleontological program.

After the Denver Museum of Natural History received DeWeese's *Diplodocus,* interest remained high, and in 1935 they traded one of their Folsom Bison skeletons for the complete skeleton of a *Diplodocus* collected at Dinosaur National Monument by the Carnegie Museum. People from the Denver Museum spent the next 2 years mounting the *Diplodocus* for display. Visitors today can still view this skeleton at the museum.

In 1937 as the *Diplodocus* was being reconstructed in the Denver Museum, the Morrison strata (layer) of Garden Park yielded another prize when a nearly complete skeleton of *Stegosaurus* was discovered. This specimen was donated to the Denver Museum, and the same crew of amateur paleontologists who mounted the *Diplodocus* began mounting the *Stegosaurus.* Their completed skeleton is on display at the museum.

In the middle 1950s the Cleveland Museum of Natural History in Cleveland, Ohio opened a quarry and spent 3 years excavating the nearly complete skeleton of a large sauropod (*Haplocanthosaurus*) which is currently on display in their museum. This skeleton was lower in the section of rocks than either the Cope or Marsh quarries and may be one of the oldest known sauropods from the Late Jurassic. In life this dinosaur was nearly 72 feet (22 meters) long. This discovery was unique because, unlike the Morrison area to the north, dinosaur fossils have been discovered in Garden Park throughout the approximately 350 feet (107 meters) of Morrison strata.

Garden Park continues to produce exciting fossils. As recently as July 1993, paleontologists from the Denver Museum of Natural History found a nest site of a two-legged ornithopod dinosaur in the Jurassic rocks. This rare nest site, 145- to 150-million years old, yielded egg fragments, a complete intact egg, and baby dinosaur fossils.

Currently a joint venture between the Bureau of Land Management (BLM), the Garden Park Paleontological Society, and the Denver Museum of Natural History is under way with plans to develop the area as a public educational resource. Long range plans call for assessing the remaining paleontological merit of the area and erecting signs and markers to point out the historical aspects of this unique area.

A second site, just north of the present day town of Morrison, Colorado, was discovered by Arthur Lakes, a clergyman and teacher. As a teacher, Lakes had impressive credentials, being formally trained in both theology and natural history at Oxford University in England. While teaching at a parochial school in Golden, Lakes pursued his interest in natural history by collecting fossils, studying the local geology and sketching and painting his discoveries and the local scenery (Figure 6).

Figure 6. Arthur Lakes' painting of a scene which may have occurred when the Morrison Formation was being deposited. It features an *Allosaurus* feeding on the carcass of a sauropod dinosaur.

On a day in March 1877, Lakes was on a rocky slope just east of what in the future would be Red Rocks Park. Like Ormel Lucas, Lakes was searching for plant fossils. Instead of fossil plants, his search was rewarded with the discovery of a large fossilized dinosaur vertebra and another large bone which would prove to be a front leg bone, both from the large sauropod, *Apatosaurus* (*Brontosaurus*). Because of his training and love of natural history Lakes knew that paleontologists from the east coast would be interested in his discovery. He quickly dispatched a letter with sketches of the bones to paleontologist Othniel Charles Marsh. His first attempt to contact Marsh proved futile, and even his second, third and fourth elicited no response. Lakes must have been a tenacious individual, for after his fourth attempt in May of 1877, he packed up over 1 ton of dinosaur bones and shipped them via railroad to Marsh. This in itself probably grabbed Marsh's attention, but the discovery that Lakes had both written and then shipped some bones to his rival, Edward Drinker Cope, spurred Marsh to action. Marsh quickly wired one of his chief field people, Benjamin Mudge, who was collecting fossils in Kansas. Marsh had Mudge travel to Golden, Colorado to investigate Lakes' discoveries. Mudge's report to Marsh was indeed glowing and substantiated Lakes' claim of the abundance of dinosaur fossils.

Marsh retained Lakes to help with the excavation south of

Figure 7. An aerial view looking south along the Dakota Hogback—a resistant series of sedimentary rocks that were initially deposited during the Mesozoic Era and were subsequently uplifted and tilted as the present day Rocky Mountains began to form.

Golden near Morrison. During the next 3 years Lakes and the Peabody Museum crew opened ten quarries along the ridge between the town of Morrison and what is today the Interstate 70 roadcut (Figure 7). Five of the quarries proved to contain dinosaur bones and many fossilized bones were shipped back to the Peabody Museum for Marsh to study. Marsh curtailed his operations near Morrison when word came to him of a site in Wyoming called Como Bluff where a 7-mile-long (11.3 kilometers) exposure of the Morrison Formation was found to contain an abundance of fossilized dinosaur bones.

Both Garden Park and a portion of the Dakota Hogback between Interstate 70 and Morrison, Colorado, now referred to as Dinosaur Ridge, are historically significant dinosaur collecting areas. Although

more then 100 years have passed since the excavation began, the dinosaurs that Cope and Marsh extracted from the Jurassic Morrison Formation represent some of the best specimens that scientists have on two of the six generally recognized suborders (groups) of dinosaurs. One group is the huge four-footed plant-eating (herbivorous) sauropods, such as *Apatosaurus* (*Brontosaurus*); another is the herbivorous plated dinosaurs (stegosaurids), such as *Stegosaurus*.

After an initial flurry of activity near Morrison, the area was to lie dormant until 1937 when a road crew unearthed another startling discovery as they were constructing Alameda Parkway, or State Highway 26, over the hogback. As the heavy machinery cut a path on the eastern, or Denver slope of the hogback, they unearthed a series of dinosaur footprints on top of a sandstone layer which represented a beach around 110-million years ago. Mountain building activity that uplifted the present day Rocky Mountains was responsible for raising this ancient beach over 1-mile high and tilting it to a present day angle of over 45 degrees. Harvey Markman, Curator of Geology at the Denver Museum of Natural History, arrived upon the scene to document the discovery, but the tracks were not studied in detail until 1986 when Dr. Martin Lockley, a geology professor at the University of Colorado at Denver, began to study the tracks. Since then Lockley and his group, the University of Colorado at Denver Dinosaur Trackers Research Group, have been involved in studying these and other tracks throughout the state. At Dinosaur Ridge, Lockley's group has documented tracks from both herbivorous and carnivorous dinosaurs that walked on the beach 110-million years ago.

This unique site west of Denver still offers an opportunity to learn about past and present day research related to dinosaurs. In 1989 the Friends of Dinosaur Ridge incorporated as a nonprofit group to protect and develop this unique educational resource, which will be further developed as Dinosaur Ridge. In the short distance of about 3.5 miles (6 kilometers) from the town of Morrison north to the Interstate 70 roadcut, visitors may examine bones in rocks of the Jurassic Morrison Formation on the west side of the ridge. On the east side of Dinosaur Ridge, fossils such as leaf impressions and many

trace fossils, including worm burrows and dinosaur tracks, can be seen. The bones and tracks can be found along the Alameda Parkway (Colorado Highway 26) which traverses the ridge. The Colorado State Highway Department has erected a fence to protect the dinosaur footprints that remain along the roadside.

Not far to the south of Dinosaur Ridge, at a construction site in the Columbine Knolls subdivision, bones and teeth of a *Tyrannosaurus rex* were found in Late Cretaceous rocks in May 1993. The remains were taken to the Denver Museum of Natural History for preparation. These are the first fossils of *Tyrannosaurus rex* uncovered in Colorado.

In 1887 another Colorado fossil discovery again focused attention on Colorado. At that time Othniel Marsh received some massive fossilized horn cores which Whitman

Cross, a U.S. Government geologist, had discovered while investigating an area east and north of Dinosaur Ridge. The rocks Cross was studying were referred to as the Denver Beds and Cross felt sure that they were quite old and was surprised to learn that Marsh identified the horn cores as those from a large bison which had lived during the Ice Age. By his own work Cross was sure the Denver Beds were deposited when dinosaurs roamed the earth. Fortunately a similar set of horn cores, this time with the rest of the skull, was discovered the same year in northeast Wyoming. After studying the Wyoming fossil, Marsh quickly realized the horn cores from the Denver Beds were not from an extinct bison, but from a new type of horned dinosaur. Thus this set of horn cores from Colorado was the first discovery of a new group of

Figure 8. Humerus (upper front-leg bone) of *Brachiosaurus altithorax* discovered by Elmer Riggs near Grand Junction. In the background is the Uncompahgre Plateau with Triassic rocks resting directly on Precambrian rocks (the darker-colored ones near the base of the cliffs). This site, now called Riggs Hill, is preserved and open to the public (see Chapter 9 for more information).

horned dinosaurs, the ceratopsians. A well-known example of this group is Triceratops.

GREAT DISCOVERIES NEAR GRAND JUNCTION AND DELTA

More new dinosaur fossils awaited discovery when people from the Field Museum of Natural History in Chicago, at that time the Field Columbian Museum, decided to mount an expedition to the state in 1899. Elmer Riggs was Assistant Paleontologist for the museum and was in charge of the project. His first act in 1899 was to send out letters of inquiry to towns along the rail lines. Knowing how heavy fossilized dinosaur bones were, he decided to confine his search to the railroad routes where he knew shipping would be within easy reach. Riggs' inquiries were rewarded with a letter from Dr. Samuel M. Bradbury, a dentist and then president of the Western Colorado Academy of Science in Grand Junction. Bradbury told Riggs about local residents who had been collecting dinosaur bones as curios since 1885. Riggs was intrigued with the report, but by the time he received Bradbury's letter, he was already committed to fieldwork in Wyoming for the 1899 field season.

In the spring of 1900 Riggs arrived in Grand Junction to begin his field work. His first season of collecting yielded the partial skeleton of *Brachiosaurus altithorax*, a large herbivorous sauropod (Figure 8). At the time, this discovery was the world's largest dinosaur and the discovery received abundant press coverage for the Field Museum.

Figure 9. Members of the Field Museum expedition to western Colorado load plaster-jacketed dinosaur bones onto a ferry across the Colorado River near Grand Junction.

Work to obtain the dinosaur fossils was arduous and at times dynamite was used to remove the overlying rocks. After the bones were exposed they were wrapped in a plaster jacket and moved by wagon and, in some cases, a ferry across the Colorado River to the railroad station (Figure 9). Riggs and his crew returned in the spring of 1901 and in the span of 2 years they opened several quarries (Figure 10) and shipped tons of large dinosaur bones back to the Field Museum. The most complete find was the partial skeleton of *Apatosaurus excelsus*, another sauropod, which was mounted in the Field Museum utilizing the bones found in the

Figure 10. Location of some of the dinosaur quarries opened by Elmer Riggs during his 1900 and 1901 expeditions that were sponsored by the Field Museum of Natural History.

quarry. At the time Mr. Field, founder and benefactor of the Field Museum, was adamant about having only real material on display in his museum. This explains why the mount of the apatosaur (Figure 11) is missing the end of the tail and the front quarter of the sauropod. After Field's death, reconstructed bones for the front limbs, neck, head and tail were added. The actual tail may still be entombed in the rocks because Riggs and his crew were unable to tunnel deep enough into the hillside due to the instability of the rocks (Figure 12). Today some of these turn of the century quarries can be visited by anyone interested in retracing the steps of Riggs' discoveries (refer to Chapter 9).

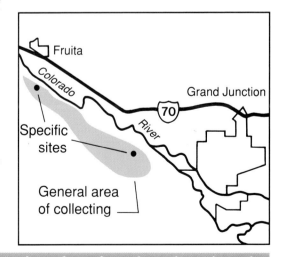

Fruita

Colorado

Grand Junction

70

River

Specific sites

General area of collecting

Figure 11. This partial skeleton of *Apatosaurus* (*Brontosaurus*) was mounted for display at the Field Museum of Natural History in Chicago in 1908. It was collected by Elmer Riggs and his crew from rocks of the Jurassic Morrison Formation at a site now called Dinosaur Hill.

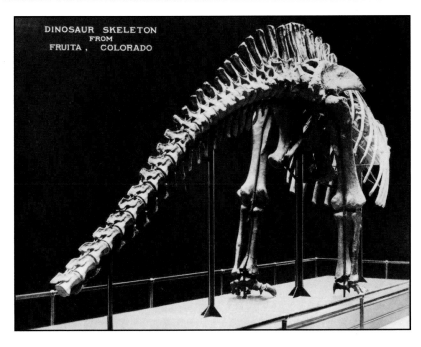

Rocks of the Morrison Formation on Colorado's Western Slope did not receive the detailed efforts of professional paleontologists again until 1964 when geologists from Brigham Young University (BYU) began to explore for dinosaur fossils. In 1968 their exploration was rewarded when they collected a nearly complete skeleton of *Camarasaurus*, a large herbivorous sauropod.

In 1971 Ed and Vivian Jones, uranium prospectors and amateur paleontologists, persuaded the BYU geologists to come to Delta, Colorado and examine dinosaur bones they had discovered many years earlier while prospecting for uranium in the Morrison Formation. The Brigham Young paleontologists found more dinosaur bones than they could deal with. This site, the Dry Mesa Dinosaur Quarry, has been worked off and on since 1972. Tons of fossilized dinosaur bones still await preparation at BYU. The most famous discoveries from this site are the giant brachiosaurid *Ultrasaurus* and diplodocid *Supersaurus*.

DEVELOPMENT OF THE NATIONAL MONUMENT TO DINOSAURS

During the early 1900s many researchers immediately thought of the states of Colorado and Wyoming when they discussed dinosaur collecting and planned expeditions. In 1908 the state of Utah was added to the list when paleontologists from the Carnegie Museum of Natural History in Pittsburgh, Pennsylvania were searching for dinosaur fossils in the Jurassic rocks of northwestern Colorado and northeastern Utah. Their explorations were rewarded when they made a significant discovery in Utah about 11 miles from the Colorado border. Today the old Carnegie quarry and approximately 330-square miles of rugged and

Figure 12. The remains of a tunnel at Dinosaur Hill dug by Elmer Riggs during his 1900 and 1901 field seasons can still be seen south of Fruita, Colorado (see Figure 10).

scenic terrain of the Uinta Mountains surrounding the quarry are managed by the National Park Service as Dinosaur National Monument. Although the dinosaur quarry lies in Utah, most of the 330 square miles of monument land is in Moffat County, Colorado. The small town of Dinosaur, Colorado lies south of the Dinosaur National Monument in Moffat County.

Dinosaur National Monument and the surrounding area first came to the attention of scientists in 1871 when the geologist and explorer John Wesley Powell, most famous for his exploration of the Grand Canyon in Arizona, reported "reptilian remains" in the area of Dinosaur National Monument. In 1893 a field party from the American Museum in New York City again noted the presence of dinosaur bones in the Jurassic Morrison Formation of northwestern Colorado and northeastern Utah. It was not until 1908 that dinosaur fossils would be rediscovered and in subsequent years quarried, but alas these bones would also leave the area, destined again for the eastern seaboard of the United States. Fortunately, these bones are on display today as reconstructed skeletons at the Carnegie Museum of Natural History in Pittsburgh, Pennsylvania.

In the summer of 1908 Earl Douglass, a vertebrate paleontologist whose specialty was ancient mammals, had been with the Carnegie Museum for 6 years and was concentrating on a search for ancient mammal fossils in north-

west Colorado and northeast Utah. He explored in northeastern Utah in the Uinta Basin, where numerous fossil mammal bones continue to be discovered. During the field season Douglass was visited by the then director of the Carnegie Museum, Dr. William J. Holland. During an evening discussion Holland and Douglass were discussing the fact that the famous Hayden Territorial Surveys had noted the presence of Jurassic rocks along the south flank of the Uinta Mountains. These rocks were just north of their campsite, so the next day Holland and Douglass took a light mule-drawn wagon and headed out to explore for dinosaur bones in these multi-colored rocks. When they arrived at the site they found the landscape riddled with steep ravines so they split up, both agreeing to signal each other with a gunshot if they found anything. Douglass was the first to fire a shot and Holland quickly headed toward Douglass who had found a femur (thigh bone) from *Diplodocus*, a herbivorous (plant eating) sauropod characteristic of the Jurassic. Unfortunately, the femur, although well preserved, was at the bottom of a steep ravine and was also too heavy for the two men to lift. Another problem presented itself when the scholars could not find the rock layer from which the bone had eroded.

During the spring of 1909, Douglass returned to the locality and enlisted the aid of George Goodrich, a local Mormon elder. Through the

pleasant spring and into the heat of summer, Douglass and Goodrich traveled up and down the steep ravines as they scoured the rocks of the Jurassic Morrison Formation in search of bone-bearing strata. Although they found many bone fragments, it was not until August 17th, according to Douglass' journal, that their search was rewarded when Douglass found eight articulated tail vertebrae from a large dinosaur high upon a resistant sandstone ridge of the upturned Morrison Formation. Douglass immediately notified Holland at the Carnegie Museum who quickly joined Douglass and began to make plans for the excavation of the site. They quickly discovered that the articulated tail vertebrae were part of the skeleton of *Apatosaurus* (*Brontosaurus*) *louisae,* a new species of a dinosaur named in honor of Mrs. Louise Carnegie, wife of Andrew Carnegie, famous industrialist, philanthropist and patron of the Carnegie Museum.

Douglass foresaw this would be an immense project involving years of time and hundreds if not thousands of hours of labor. Fortunately the project had the financial backing of Andrew Carnegie so Douglass' job was to concentrate on the removal of the bones. Early in the history of the quarry, Douglass and Holland saw the importance of not only methodically removing the bones but protecting the area as a national treasure. When they learned that the area was to be opened to homesteading they were able to convince the United States Government to set

Figure 13. A building protects the bones first unearthed by Earl Douglass at Dinosaur National Monument.

A COMMON BOND

Each of the previously discussed historical sites, Garden Park, Dinosaur Ridge, the Grand Junction area and Dinosaur National Monument, has its own unique history but all have made significant contributions to scientific understanding of the dinosaurs that roamed the earth around 153- to 137-million years ago. There is a common bond among these different localities: all have dinosaur fossils from a time when giant dinosaurs roamed the land, a time when there was little change in the landscape from Colorado to the Canadian border. Each of these sites has yielded hundreds if not thousands of dinosaur bones preserved from a remote time in the earth's history.

aside the quarry and 80 acres around it as a national monument. President Woodrow Wilson designated the area as such in 1915.

Following the discovery in 1909, crews from the Carnegie Museum excavated bones for 13 years. Douglass was in charge of the operation for the entire time. He paid careful attention to documenting the position of the thousands of bones that were removed. By the time the Carnegie crew finished their project, 350 tons (317,520 kilograms) of dinosaur bones had been shipped to the Carnegie Museum. Within this collection were enough bones to allow the reconstruction of 20 skeletons representing 10 different species of dinosaurs. Many partial skeletons and isolated bones are still in the collections.

Immediately following the Carnegie efforts the Smithsonian Institution and the University of Utah collected skeletons from the quarry. Work at the quarry then essentially ceased until 1958, when Douglass' wish to have the quarry opened to the public with the bones displayed in

place was finally fulfilled. The building was constructed with the quarry face as the north wall—a 183-foot long (56 meters) and 60-foot high (18 meters) cliff of sandstone which contains the dinosaur bones. Today people can visit the newly refurbished quarry site (Figures 13 and 14) to view the bones and learn about the Jurassic dinosaurs through many educational displays located in the building.

Figure 14. The bones at Dinosaur National Monument were left in place after the rocks which once entombed them were removed. Visitors can thus gain a feel for what it is like to find and excavate dinosaur fossils in the field.

A RECORD IN THE ROCKS

THE PROCESS OF FOSSILIZATION

HUNDREDS, IF NOT THOUSANDS, of tons of dinosaur bones have been excavated within Colorado. The reason why Colorado has such a bonanza of dinosaur fossils lies in the state's active geologic past. Millions of years ago Colorado had an ideal natural setting which helped preserve dinosaur bones. Much of the surface of Colorado was near sea level or, as was the case several times during the Mesozoic (225- to 65-million years ago), was under the sea. Sand, silt, and mud were eroded from higher ground and deposited near sea level. This setting was perfect for quick burial of the dinosaur bodies. Quick burial greatly enhances the chance that an organism will become a fossil.

A quick burial is only one of the steps involved in the process of fossilization illustrated in Figure 15. In Blocks a through c, rising flood waters quickly cover a stegosaur that has died along the river. Sediment carried by the river drops out of the water as the flood recedes and covers the carcass of the dinosaur. This simple but quick process is often complicated when dealing with vertebrate animals, or any animal that is composed of various parts. Often the process of decay, action of scav-

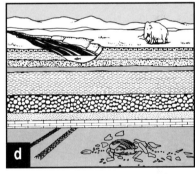

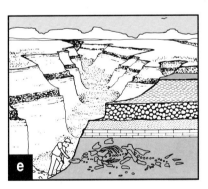

Figure 15. How a dinosaur becomes a fossil. In the process of fossilization, rapid burial is required. This happens to the *Stegosaurus* that has died near the banks of a Jurassic river (Block a). A fortuitous flood (Block b) occurs soon after the dinosaur dies. A large amount of sediment carried by river drops out of the water as the flood subsides (Block c). After millions of years during which more layers of sediment accumulate and turn to stone (Block d) the rock layer is again exposed by erosion and someone looking for fossils makes a discovery (Block e).

engers and/or the process of burial may scatter or damage the hard parts of the animal. Paleontologists are often ecstatic when they find a dinosaur with eighty percent or more of its skeleton preserved. Many museum dinosaur displays may con-

tain only 50 percent real bone. The rest of the skeleton is composed of sculpted replacement bones which have been skillfully crafted by museum technicians.

Even if the carcass of a dinosaur was quickly buried, a long series of events lies ahead. During the process of fossilization, minerals dissolved within the groundwater will often precipitate within natural cavities in the bones and strengthen them. This process adds weight to the bones by filling in many if not all of the voids within the bones. As the layers of sand mud and silt continue to build up over the dinosaur bones, they may become fractured or distorted by the increasing weight of the overlying sediments. This presents a complex problem for museum preparators who must restore the bones to their original shape.

After millions of years, something must happen to bring the fossilized skeleton of the dinosaur to the surface where it might be discovered. In Colorado, around 65-million years ago, mountain building processes driven by the collision of the continents started to uplift the land. This process took several million years and is responsible for the present day Rocky Mountains. Now that the area is high, it is undergoing erosion rather than deposition, and the process of erosion is exposing older and older rocks (see Blocks d and e of Figure 15). Although fossils are a nonrenewable resource, continual erosion brings to light many new fossils that have been entombed in the rocks for millions of years.

THE VAST SCALE OF GEOLOGIC TIME

It sounds like all of this happened just yesterday. Indeed, to geologists, who often speak in terms of millions of years, these events associated with dinosaurs did happen in the not too distant past—considering that the earth is around 4.5-*billion* years old. This concept of geologic time is difficult to understand. To better put geologic time in perspective refer to

ERA	PERIOD	MILLIONS OF YEARS AGO	CHARACTERISTIC LIFE
Cenozoic, Time of Recent Life	Quaternary	2	modern life, mankind dominates land, many large mammals become extinct and primitive man evolves
	Tertiary		mammals rapidly increase in size and variety, mammals spread to all continents, grasses appear and flowering plants become abundant
Mesozoic, Time of Middle Life	Cretaceous	65	dinosaurs and many marine animals become extinct at 65 million years largest variety of dinosaurs (horned, duckbilled, armored, iguanodontids and largest carnivores), most sauropods and plated dinosaurs become extinct early in the Cretaceous, flowering plants appear
	Jurassic	136	giant dinosaurs (sauropods) abundant, plated dinosaurs appear, first toothed birds, first lizards and crocodiles, conifers and cycads abundant, modern sharks and bony fish appear
	Triassic	193	dinosaurs evolve from thecodont reptiles, primitive mammals appear, armored amphibians and mammal-like reptiles die out
Paleozoic, Time of Early Life	Permian	225	mass extinction of many invertebrates and armored fish, primitive & mammal-like reptiles evolve, conifers (gymnosperms) evolve
	Carboniferous (Pennsylvanian/ Mississippian)	270	coal swamps with massive forests of fern trees, insects (some giant) make a sudden appearance, amphibians are the dominant life on land, first reptiles evolve
	Devonian	350	abundant fish and sharks, jawless fish die out, first invertebrates on land (crabs and land snails), first primitive land plants, first amphibians
	Silurian	400	many jawless and armored fish, extensive coral reefs and many invertebrates, first evidence of life on land
	Ordovician	440	first vertebrates (primitive fish) appear, abundant varieties of marine invertebrates with hard parts
	Cambrian	500	marine invertebrate fossils begin to appear in abundance, most types of invertebrates present by this time, many invertebrates possess hard parts, no evidence of life on land
Precambrian		600 to 4.5 Billion Years Ago	few fossils, only soft bodied marine organisms no fossils during earth's early history origin of the earth at 4.5 billion years ago

Figure 16. The geologic time scale.

Figure 16. This figure contains a scale time line of the last 600-million years of earth's history which contains the majority of fossils. To the left of the time column are the terms that geologists use to refer to the various blocks of time in the earth's history. Using these terms helps geologists and other interested people talk about various episodes in the history of life. The right hand column of Figure 16 summarizes the characteristic life that was present during a specific era or period of geologic time.

Note on Figure 16 that dinosaurs appeared on the scene about 205-million years ago during the Triassic Period, the first of three geologic periods which comprise the Mesozoic Era. Dinosaurs survived as a group until the end of the Mesozoic Era, a time span of around 140-million years of the earth's history, about one-quarter of the time line on Figure 16. This still sounds impressive, but to put the reign of the dinosaurs in perspective with the age of the earth (4.5 billion years), the scale time column would have to extended an additional 48 inches (1.25 meters) from the 600-million year boundary between the Cambrian and Precambrian on Figure 16. Although few people would argue that dinosaurs were not a successful group, their 140-million year reign is only 3.1 percent of the time that has passed since the formation of the earth.

The Mesozoic is only one of three major eras of time from which fossils are commonly preserved. The ages in ascending order are the Pale-ozoic Era (early life) or age of invertebrates, the Mesozoic Era (middle life) or Age of Reptiles and the Cenozoic Era (recent life) or Age of Mammals. A fourth interval of time, the Precambrian, marks the period of earth history when there was very primitive life. Geologists further subdivide each of the three eras into periods. Scientists assign relative ages to some rocks based on the types of fossils found within them. Actual ages of certain rocks such as lava flows, volcanic ash layers, or igneous intrusions are measured by the decay of radioactive minerals within the rocks.

MAJOR ROCK TYPES

Colorado is somewhat unique because rocks from each of the geologic periods are present at the surface. Many of the oldest rocks in the state do not contain any fossils because they have been extensively altered by heat and pressure or have crystallized from a molten state. Rocks which have cooled from a molten state are called igneous and are illustrated in Figure 17. Rocks which have been transformed by high pressures and temperatures are called metamorphic rocks and are illustrated in Figure 18. Metamorphism can alter either igneous, sedimentary, or even other pre-existing metamorphic rocks. Rocks which contain fossils are unique and are classified as sedimentary rocks. These rocks were derived from pre-existing rocks and represent gravel, sand, silt, and different types of mud that over millions of years were deposited by wind or water and solidified into rocks called sand-

Figure 17. Igneous rocks are rocks that crystallized from a molten state. Note the size of the crystals in this rock compared to the pen in the photograph.

Figure 18. An example of metamorphic rocks.

In Utah the salt flats around the Great Salt Lake are a good example of chemical precipitates.

THE MESOZOIC ERA IN COLORADO

In Colorado, the Mesozoic sedimentary rocks form a series of layers which record the existence of deserts, rivers, lakes and oceans. Geologists who study these rocks can piece together a fascinating story of the environments millions of years ago. Today, dinosaur researchers who are experts in the anatomy of dinosaurs often work closely with geologists who are proficient in analyzing past environments. Together these scientists can construct a more valid interpretation of the life and time of the

stones, siltstones, and shales. A common characteristic of sedimentary rocks is that they all exhibit layering as can be seen in sedimentary rocks of the Morrison Forma- tion, a rock unit known worldwide for its dinosaur fossils. (Figure 19). Sometimes sedimentary rocks are chemicals that have precipitated out of solution in lakes or oceans.

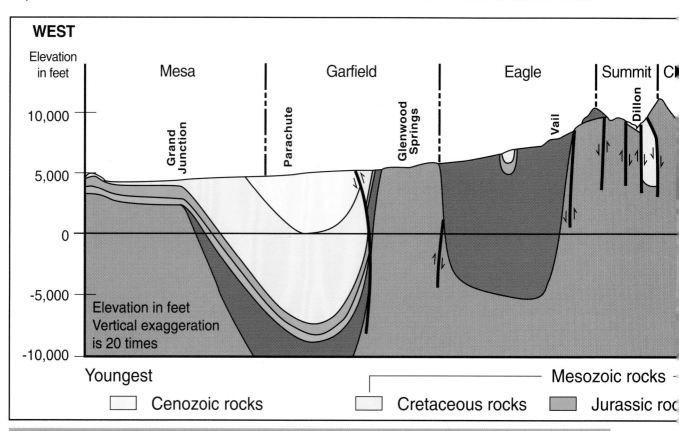

dinosaurs. Environmental conditions changed, sometimes drastically, during the 140-million year reign of the dinosaurs.

As a basis for their interpretations, experts in the study of dinosaurs and ancient environments look at the fossils found in the rocks, the types of rocks and their internal structures (such as ripple marks, cross bedding or on a larger scale channel scours). All of these data form a record of what the life and conditions of the time were like. Most of the time this record is incomplete, but as explorations continue, more data may come to light and long held interpretations may have to be changed or revised in order to conform to the new evidence.

Figure 19. An example of sedimentary rocks of the Morrison Formation west of Grand Junction in the Fruita Paleontological Area.

Figure 20. A Generalized geologic cross section from east to west along Interstate 70 in Colorado. This side view of the rocks along Interstate 70 shows the surface of the land and the configuration of the rocks of the main geologic time periods.

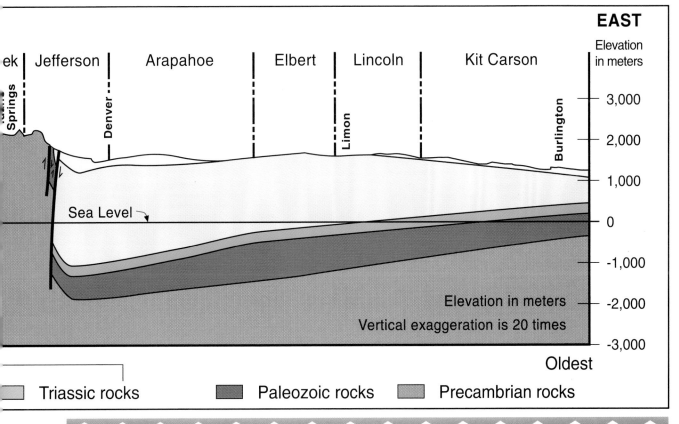

Colorado is an excellent setting to look for rocks and fossils from the Age of Reptiles because many of these rocks are today exposed at the surface. An episode of mountain building which started shortly, at least in terms of geologic time, before dinosaurs became extinct, is responsible for deforming the strata deposited during the Age of Reptiles. These Mesozoic rocks along with older and younger strata have been uplifted and downwarped by the slow but relentless forces of mountain building caused by the collision of the earth's mobile continental plates.

Figure 20 presents a present-day cross-sectional view of the rock layers along Interstate 70. Imagine that Interstate 70 is the trace of a knife across Colorado which is a cake. If a vertical slice is made in the cake the various layers will be exposed along the cut. In essence, this is what this figure illustrates. It is based upon a study of the rocks at the surface and the same rock layers that occur below the surface in oil wells. Figure 20 graphically shows Precambrian rocks which have been uplifted to form the core of the present day Rocky Mountains. These rocks are visible along Interstate 70 through Summit County, Colorado. To the west and east of Summit County the rocks have been uplifted and downwarped resulting in the present day exposure of many rocks from the Mesozoic (Age of Reptiles). The downwarped areas in western Garfield County and eastern Jefferson and all of Arapahoe County are called basins. These basins contain Colorado's oil and gas resources.

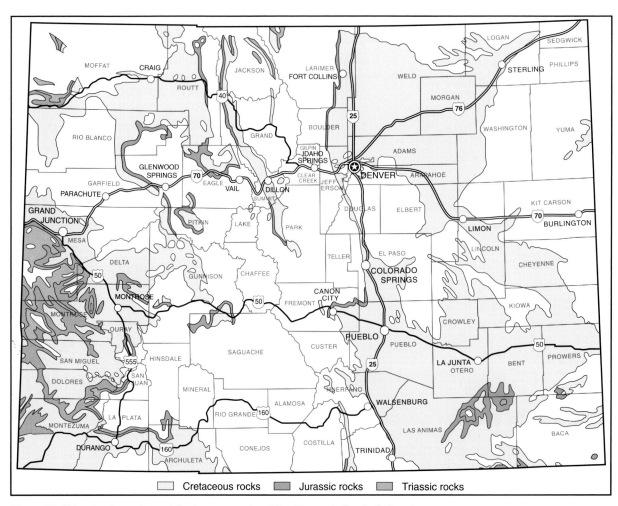

Figure 21. Triassic, Jurassic, and Cretaceous rocks of the Mesozoic Era in Colorado.

During the past 65 million years some of the rocks have been uplifted in excess of 15,000 feet (4,752 meters). This may seem like a large amount but it averages to a little over .00024 inches (.0061 millimeters) per year. The uplifts and downwarps associated with mountain building are usually much more dramatic than a slow continual event. Often they occur as abrupt movements that quickly release built up stresses resulting from the collision and splitting apart of continental masses. These abrupt movements are along faults and they can easily shift the earth's surface by a few inches to several feet at a time. Most of the mountain building in Colorado took place during the early part of the Cenozoic (Age of Mammals or recent life) and is responsible for bringing Mesozoic rocks to the surface. Colorado probably shook like California often does today as the Rocky Mountains were pushed up to their present day heights. By the time Native Americans and early settlers started to live in the state, mountain building had slowed dramatically and dinosaur fossils had been eroding from the rocks for thousands of years. Many fossils weathered to dust long before the first humans visited the area.

Mesozoic rocks that today occur at the surface cover over one-third of Colorado (Figure 21). Major rock units which contain either body and/or trace fossils of dinosaurs are shown in Figure 22 which is referred to as a geologic column. Geologists describe a geo-

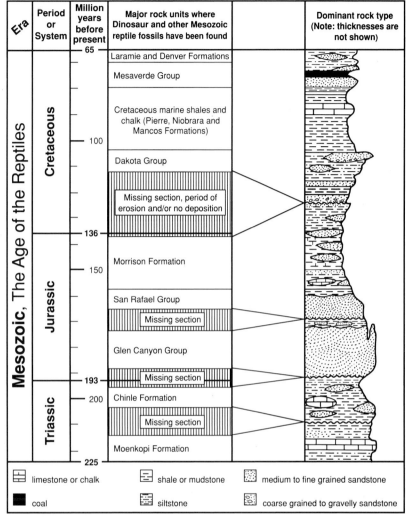

Figure 22. A columnar section which shows the Mesozoic Era by age of the rocks, types of rock deposited, and names given to each specific rock unit. Missing time intervals are shown as a wavy line on the drawing of the rock type and are indicated again on the chart of the major rock units.

logic column in ascending order, studying the oldest to the youngest. Note that the oldest rock unit on the column is the Moenkopi Formation which is Triassic in age. Immediately above the Moenkopi is a wavy line on the dominant rock type column and an interval marked "missing section" in the column with the major rock units. These annota-

tions tell geologists that deposition was not continuous through time and that the indicated time interval is missing in the area where the rock column was described. It may be missing either to due to erosion, never being deposited in the area, or a combination of erosion and nondeposition. Thus in Colorado the rocks of the Moenkopi Formation are directly in contact with the overlying, and hence younger, rocks of the Chinle Formation. Approximately 5-million years of the earth's history is missing.

ROCK FORMATIONS THAT YIELD DINOSAUR FOSSILS

Dinosaur fossils are most common in the following rocks: the Late Triassic Chinle Formation, the Late Jurassic Morrison Formation, the Early Cretaceous Dakota Group, the Late Cretaceous Mesaverde Group and the Laramie and Denver Formations. In the other units shown on Figure 22 dinosaur fossils are a rare occurrence, but in some cases, fossils of other reptiles that lived alongside the dinosaurs are more common. This is the case for the marine shales and chalks of the Cretaceous where mosasaurs and plesiosaurs, both sea going reptiles, have been found.

The lowermost, and oldest, rock unit which contains dinosaur fossils on Figure 22 is the Chinle Formation which is Late Triassic in age. In Colorado these rocks contain the tracks of small dinosaurs which lived during Late Triassic time. Rocks of the Chinle are best known from Arizona where they comprise the famous Painted Desert and have a wealth of fossils of Late Triassic plant and animal life.

Next youngest and best known for its dinosaur fossils is the world-famous Morrison Formation. These rocks, were deposited on a large, low flatland about 137- to 153-million years ago. Besides being famous for dinosaur fossils, the Jurassic Morrison Formation is well known for its

Figure 23. An example of Morrison Formation rocks located west of Grand Junction.

uranium resources. The layers and lenses of sandstone that represent sand bars and channel fills of long-dried up rivers and streams often contain rich deposits of uranium. Around Grand Junction on Colorado's Western Slope prospecting for uranium has often resulted in the discovery of dinosaur fossils, especially during the 1950s when the area was explored heavily.

Characteristically the rocks of the Morrison Formation are distinguished by their wide variety of colors. When viewed from afar, the mudstones, siltstones, sandstones and thin limestone deposits look like a multi-colored layer cake with light-burgundy, gray-green, gray-and buff-colored horizons (Figure 23). The sandstone layers are more resistant to erosion and often form step-like ledges or isolated pods of sandstone within this multi-colored formation. Dinosaur fossils have come from vir-

tually every type of rock within the Morrison Formation. Fossilized bones are the most common type of fossil found, but footprints and even a fossilized nest with eggs have been discovered within the Morrison.

Another missing time interval marks the contact between the underlying Morrison Formation and the next youngest unit, the Dakota Group (see Figure 22). Rocks of the Dakota Group are Cretaceous in age and are dominated by yellowish-tan to buff-colored sandstones which often contain many trace fossils and sedimentary structures such as ripple marks. These rocks are thick, massive, continuous and a ridge-forming unit (Figure 24). The shales which separate the sandstones are gray and weather easily to a fine powder. These rocks mark the first incursion of a large Cretaceous seaway which flooded Colorado, then receded only to return and flood Colorado several

Figure 24. Rocks of the Cretaceous Dakota Group, here tilted on end along Interstate 70 west of Denver, are tan sandstones interlayered with gray shales. All of these rocks were once flat lying, but mountain building forces, which reached their zenith in Colorado after dinosaurs became extinct, tilted these rocks into the present configuration.

times during the Cretaceous. The main dinosaur fossils found are a wide variety of footprints, both in the form of isolated footprints and trackways. These trace fossils record the coming and going of both herbivorous and carnivorous dinosaurs. Only a few isolated dinosaur bones have been found so it is not known for sure what specific dinosaurs were roaming the state at this time.

After its first incursion into Colorado during the early part of the Cretaceous, the seaway continued to invade more of the state. This shallow inland sea inundated Colorado until the Late Cretaceous when the water began to recede and land once more was above sea level. It was at this time that rocks of the Mesaverde Group were deposited, around 80-million years ago. These rocks are interbedded light-tan sandstones, gray shales, and coal (Figure 25). Dinosaur fossils within the Mesaverde consist of footprints and trackways commonly visible in the roofs of coal mines after the coal has been mined. A few dinosaur bones and

Figure 25. Interbedded sandstones, siltstones, shales, and coal of the Mesaverde Group exposed in the Trapper Mine located south of the town Craig in northwest Colorado.

partial skeletons have been discovered in the Mesaverde. Only now are the fossils starting to be explored by Dr. David Archibald and his students from San Diego State University in California (see Chapter 8 for more details).

Rocks of the Mesaverde are very distinctive because they form the first distinct ledges and cliffs which lie immediately above the more gentle, often gray slopes. The tan sandstones and siltstones of the Mesaverde are more resistant. When viewed from a distance the ledges and cliffs look like the pages of a book. Indeed in the classic exposures near Grand Junction they are referred to as the Book Cliffs. Rocks of the Mesaverde Group are quite extensive in western Colorado.

Near the end of the Cretaceous, mountain building processes had uplifted Colorado enough to push the inland sea out of the state. Two rock formations were deposited in the eastern half of the state which record the Late Cretaceous heyday of the dinosaurs and their subsequent extinction. These two rock units are the Laramie and Denver Formations. Neither of these formations have been tilted and deformed as much as the rocks of the Morrison Formation, Dakota Group and Mesaverde Group. The Laramie and Denver Formations occur on the plains in the eastern half of the state as nearly flat lying rock layers.

Rocks of the Laramie Formation are a series of shales, claystones, sandstones, coal beds and volcanic ash which were deposited in a lowland with coal swamps and sluggishly moving rivers. They contain the last evidence of an area which was a lowland. Rocks of the Denver Formation immediately overlie the Laramie and contain more sandstone and no coal. Hence these rocks were deposited in a more uplifted setting. Interbedded lava flows within the Denver Formation (Figure 26) attest to an uplift which was very active at this time. Some of these flows have been dated at between 62 and 64 million years old. These lava flows may be seen east of Lookout Mountain on the table mountains. All of these sites are near the town of Golden, Colorado, the home of the Colorado School of Mines and the Coors Brewery. The Denver Formation is unique because the lower portion contains dinosaur fossils and the upper part contains primitive Tertiary mammals and abundant plant fossils.

Figure 26. Rocks of the Denver Formation viewed from Lookout Mountain toward Golden.

DEFINING THE BEASTS

PROBLEMS WITH CLASSIFICATION

Today the scientific classification of dinosaurs is in a state of flux. Some scientists argue that dinosaurs should be in a class by themselves, the dinosauria, equal in status to mammals and reptiles. In this scenario birds would be considered as part of the dinosauria. (It is now widely accepted that birds evolved from a line of dinosaurs sometime in the Jurassic Period.) Other scientists still want to class dinosaurs as reptiles. Fossil evidence from the nearly 300 valid genera of dinosaurs can be used to support either argument.

Before discussing some details of classification it may be best to define the concept of a dinosaur. A true definition of a dinosaur (literally terrible lizard) is a list of criteria that a majority of researchers have agreed to. Dinosaurs do have a major tie with the reptiles because many dinosaurs are known to have laid eggs. Some dinosaur skeletons have been found in association with eggs. Nests with fossilized baby dinosaurs, both in and out of their eggs, have been discovered. A few researchers argue that some dinosaurs may have given birth to live young, but overwhelming evidence indicates dinosaurs laid eggs. Because soft body anatomy is generally not pre-

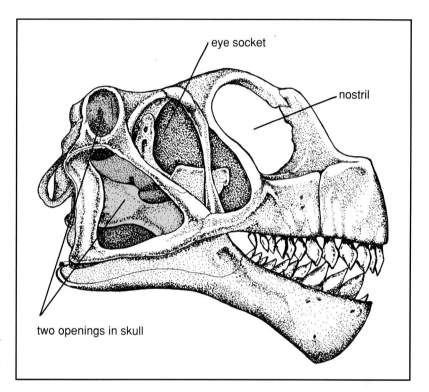

Figure 27. Skull of a typical dinosaur showing the two openings in the back.

served in the fossil record, we will probably never know if some dinosaurs reproduced by giving birth to live young. It should be noted that live birth and egg laying are characteristics of mammals and birds, respectively.

Other general criteria apply to dinosaurs. The dinosaurs discussed in this book are extinct, living during the Mesozoic Era. No aquatic dinosaur fossil has ever been found, although in rare cases dinosaur fossils have been found in rocks

deposited in the ocean. Mesozoic marine rocks do contain the fossils of large marine reptiles that lived in the shallow Mesozoic oceans. These seagoing reptiles had a completely different skeletal structure, especially in the skull and the bones of the backbone.

All dinosaurs have certain aspects of their skeleton in common. Dinosaurs have two openings in the back of their skull which in life served as attachment areas for muscles, thus giving the jaw added strength (Figure 27). Most reptiles of today possess these openings. This fact is often cited by researchers who favor classifying dinosaurs as reptiles. Dinosaurs also have their legs tucked pillar like and straight under their body like mammals, such as a dog or elephant.

Many scientists still argue for classing dinosaurs as reptiles, literally translated as "one that crawls." This translation alone points out some of the problems currently associated with dinosaur classification, especially since dinosaurs had their legs tucked under their bodies, not in the sprawling stance seen in many of today's reptiles. No matter what school of thought scientists adhere to, all dinosaurs are classified according to the Linnaean classification system. The Linnaean system of biological classification was developed by Swedish botanist Carl von Linné to show relationships between living members of the plant and animal kingdoms. This system is also applied to the fossil record. Problems have arisen because the Linnaean system makes use of soft body anatomy and the capacity for interbreeding to establish relationships. In the fossil record it is nearly impossible to study these facets of an extinct organism. Soft body parts are rarely preserved and breeding between extinct animals or plants can not be studied for obvious reasons.

Everyone who has studied dinosaurs does agree that there were two basic types, the saurischians, or

lizard-hipped dinosaurs, and the ornithischians, or bird-hipped dinosaurs. In the Linnaean system these two types of dinosaurs are called Order Saurischia and Order Ornithischia. These two orders contain as many as 57 different families of dinosaurs. The hip structure and a few examples of the many varieties of saurischian and ornithischian dinosaurs are illustrated in Figure 28. As shown in the illustration, bird-hipped dinosaurs have a pelvis or hip where the three bones that make up the pelvis (ilium, ischium and pubis) are parallel or subparallel to the backbone of the dinosaur. In the lizard-hipped

dinosaurs the ischium and pubis are at an acute angle to the backbone. When viewed from the side the saurischian pelvis has a tripod like look to it. Although many dinosaurs appeared and vanished during the Mesozoic, both saurischian and ornithischian dinosaurs lived side by side during their 140-million year history. An interesting sidelight to this classification scheme is that all ornithischian dinosaurs were herbivorous (plant eating) while the saurischians are comprised of both herbivores and carnivores (meat eaters).

Figure 28. Hip structures of typical saurischian (top two dinosaurs) and ornithischian (bottom four dinosaurs).

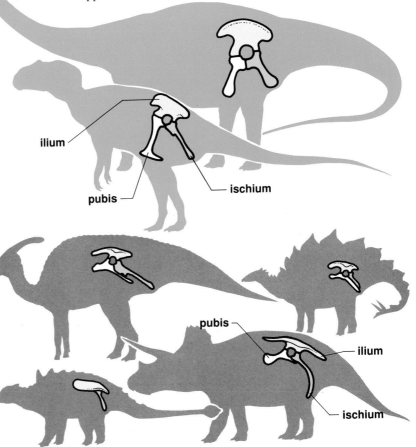

ilium

pubis

ischium

pubis

ilium

ischium

THECODONTS—THE COMMON ANCESTOR

All dinosaurs had a common ancestor the thecodont (rooted tooth) reptiles from the Triassic Period. Thecodonts were a short lived reptilian phenomena and were not a large part of the land fauna until late in the Triassic. They appeared during the Late Permian on a landscape dominated by mammal-like and other reptiles including the ancestors of present day lizards. Thecodonts underwent rapid evolution in the Triassic, as the mammal-like reptiles were becoming extinct. In turn, the thecodonts were replaced by dinosaurs by the end of the Triassic period. During the 32-million years of the Triassic thecodonts not only spawned the two orders of dinosaurs, but also pterosaurs (flying reptiles) and crocodilians. Four main types of thecodonts existed and most members of the group were predators (Figure 29). One type, the phytosaurs (Figure 29a), were large crocodile-like carnivores which occupied the same ecologic niche as today's crocodilians. Although they superficially resembled alligators and crocodiles (refer to Figure 29a and Figure 44 in Chapter 5), an obvious difference was that phytosaurs had their nostrils immediately in front of their eyes rather than on the end of their long narrow snout which is seen in today's crocodilians. Phytosaurs were the largest of the thecodont clan, reaching lengths of nearly 12 feet (3.6 meters).

A second group of thecodonts called pseudosuchians, possessed

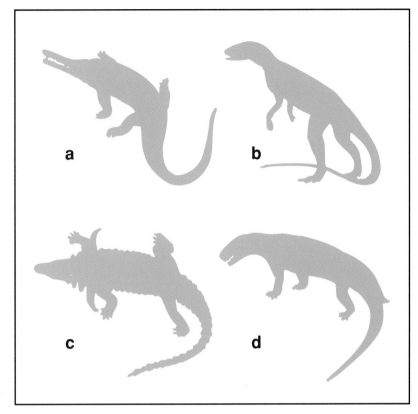

Figure 29. Four common types of thecodonts that lived during the Triassic Period: a) a phytosaur, b) a typical pseudosuchian, c) an aetosaur, and d) a typical proterosuchian.

many characteristics similar to dinosaurs (Figure 29b). All of these were rather small in size, often less than half the size of the larger phytosaurs. They all shared a rather unique leg and hip socket arrangement which allowed them to walk partially erect. In effect these reptiles were capable of a variable gait, they could walk on all fours with splayed legs like present day reptiles, or could pull themselves erect with their legs nearly under their bodies for a quick bipedal dash. The ankle joint of these reptiles was also much stronger and able to better support the animal once it pulled itself erect. Because these reptiles were preda-

tors, this may have been an adaptation for quickly running down their prey, either other small reptiles or insects of that time. Most researchers agree that this group gave rise to the dinosaurs around 205-million years ago during the Late Triassic.

A third group of thecodonts, called aetosaurs, were heavily armored with bony plates covering their back and in some cases their bellies (Figure 29c). All members of this group were quadrupedal (walked on all fours) and appear to have been herbivores. Fossils of the aetosaurs can be a common occurrence in rocks of Triassic age. These animals may not have been more

Figure 30. Footprints of the hind foot of a sauropod (a) and an allosaurid (b), both from the Jurassic age Morrison Formation in southeastern Colorado and the hind footprint of an iguanodontid dinosaur (c) from rocks of the Cretaceous Period, Dakota Group west of Denver.

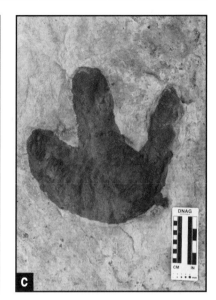

abundant than other animals of the time, but because their bodies were heavily armored with bony plates, they were a good candidate for becoming part of the fossil record. Other unarmored and more lightly built thecodonts did not stand as good a chance for becoming fossils. These animals became extinct by the end of this 32-million-year long geologic period.

A more heavily built quadrupedal predator rounds out the varieties of thecodonts present during the Triassic (Figure 29d). This group, called the proterosuchians, were the most primitive of the thecodonts and showed no tendency toward a bipedal stance. Other primitive traits include the presence of palatal teeth, teeth on the roof of the mouth. Fossils of these the-

codonts are not as abundant as those of the other groups, and like the aetosaurs, these thecodonts became extinct at the end of the Triassic and did not leave any descendants.

Early dinosaurs which evolved during the Late Triassic were quite small in comparison to the gigantic dinosaurs which are characteristic of the Jurassic period. Probably the most significant evolutionary advance was

that most of the early dinosaurs were bipedal. In Colorado the fossil evidence of these early dinosaurs consists of footprints in the Triassic rocks on the state's Western Slope. These tracks are only part of a wide variety of dinosaur fossils which researchers use to categorize the many different types of dinosaurs which lived and died during the 145-million year reign of this large and varied group.

Figure 31. Dinosaur bones that have been excavated for public display at Dinosaur National Monument which is located in western Colorado and eastern Utah.

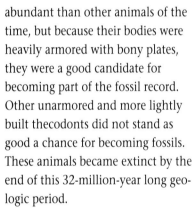

CHAPTER FOUR

The fossils which scientists use can be of two types, either trace fossils (Figure 30) such as footprints or skin impressions, or body fossils including bones and teeth. Hard parts are most commonly found and soft body parts are generally not preserved. In some rare cases the stomach contents of dinosaurs, in the form of fossilized plant material in herbivores and fossilized bones of the prey in carnivores, have been discovered. Both trace and body fossils give clues about the anatomy or appearance of the dinosaur (Figure 31) and its behavior. Trace fossils are unique in that they offer clues about how dinosaurs moved around in their world.

MAJOR GROUPS AND SUBGROUPS

Literally thousands of descriptions of various dinosaur fossils form the basis for dividing dinosaurs into two large orders, the saurischians and ornithischians. The saurischians and ornithischians are further divided into six different subgroups (Figure 32). Dinosaurs from all of these groups have been found in the Mesozoic rocks in Colorado. Each of the six subgroups of dinosaurs have their own distinguishing characteristics which set them apart or link them to other dinosaurs which have been discovered.

Saurischian or Lizard-Hipped Dinosaurs

Sauropods

The most abundant dinosaurs from Colorado's past are the giant four-footed herbivores which form a large group called the sauropods. Representatives of this subgroup were the first dinosaurs to be found and described by both Edward D. Cope and Othniel C. Marsh after their excavations of 1877 along Colorado's Front Range. Bones of these giants were also the first ones discovered by Elmer Riggs as he started excavation near Grand Junction in 1900. Sauropod bones were also the

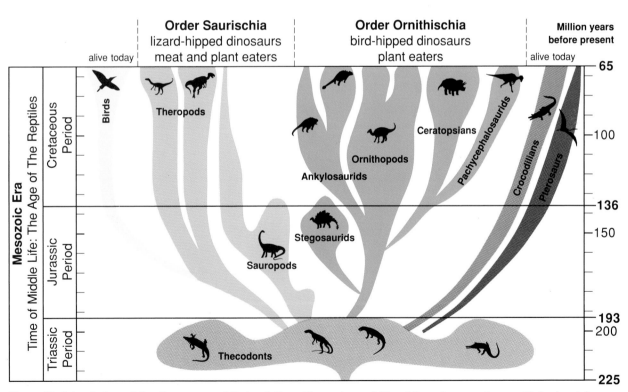

Figure 32. A family tree of the dinosaurs and their relatives. The various widths of the subgroups (ones with horizontal names) show the relative abundance compared to other groups and how fast each one spread and then declined throughout the Mesozoic Era.

first to be found by Earl Douglass as he started excavations at Dinosaur National Monument in 1909.

One of the most distinguishing characteristics of the sauropods is their long neck and tail (Figure 33). Teeth of these dinosaurs were either simple peg-like structures as seen in *Diplodocus* and *Apatosaurus* (*Brontosaurus*) or they may have been spoon shaped as seen in *Brachiosaurus* and *Camarasaurus* (Figure 34). They probably used these simple teeth to strip vegetation from the trees upon which they fed. During life they may have filled the ecologic niche of today's giraffes. As is indicated, all members of this suborder were vegetarians, and they possessed the saurischian style of pelvis. There may be as many as six different families of sauropods that lived at one time or another during the Mesozoic. Sauropods hold the distinction of being the giants of the dinosaur world. Members of this group hold the record for attaining the largest size of any living land animal. As far as size goes Colorado's dinosaurs are close to holding the record. Mesa County, Colorado has the distinction of being the only county in the United States where bones from the

second, third and fourth largest dinosaurs in the world have been found. In decreasing size these are *Ultrasaurus*, *Supersaurus* and *Brachiosaurus*.

Both *Ultrasaurus* and *Brachiosaurus* are brachiosaurids (literally arm lizards, Figure 33), dinosaurs characterized by a short faced skull with spoon shaped teeth, nostrils on the top of the skull, a long neck, short but massive body and a long and stout tail. *Ultrasaurus*, the world's second largest dinosaur, may have been as tall as three giraffes (about 60 feet or 18.3 meters tall). Its cousin *Brachiosaurus* reached a height of 40 feet (12.2 meters). *Brachiosaurus* was also first discovered in Mesa County.

Supersaurus is currently the world's third largest dinosaur and is a diplodocid, or a cousin of *Apatosaurus* (*Brontosaurus*) and *Diplodocus*. These dinosaurs are characterized by their long almost horse-like head, extremely long, slender necks and tails and a body

that is longer and thinner than brachiosaurids. In general sauropods are a common fossil in the Jurassic.

Theropods

Not all saurischian dinosaurs were gigantic four-footed herbivores. Other members of this group were fleet-footed agile carnivores or perhaps omnivores and belong to the second major group of saurischian dinosaurs, the theropods (beast foot, Figure 35). Some of the dinosaurs in this group were very small and lightly built, such as *Echinodon*, a Jurassic dinosaur found in the Morrison Formation in western Colorado which was the size of a chicken (2 feet, or 60 centimeters). Other theropods ranged in size to up to the gigantic *Tyrannosaurus rex* which towered over 18 feet (12 meters) in height and reached a length of 39 feet (12 meters).

Figure 33. A Side view of the skeleton of a *Brachiosaurus*, one of the sauropod dinosaurs. The 6-foot-high plant in the illustration is a cycad, used here for scale. Cycads were common throughout the Mesozoic Era.

6 feet or
1.8 meters

Figure 34. Peg-like tooth of a diplodocid (left) and the more spoon shaped tooth (right) of a brachiosaurid.

There are many different types of theropods which are divided into two major infraorders (Figure 32). One contingent, the coelurosaurs (hollow tail lizards) characteristically have hollow bones like birds. Some share another bird-like characteristic by not having any teeth. Like some of today's birds coelurosaurids may have been omnivores (eating both plants and animals). Other coelurosaurs possessed serrated dagger-like teeth commonly associated with the dinosaurs of prey. Coelurosaurs were bipedal, probably

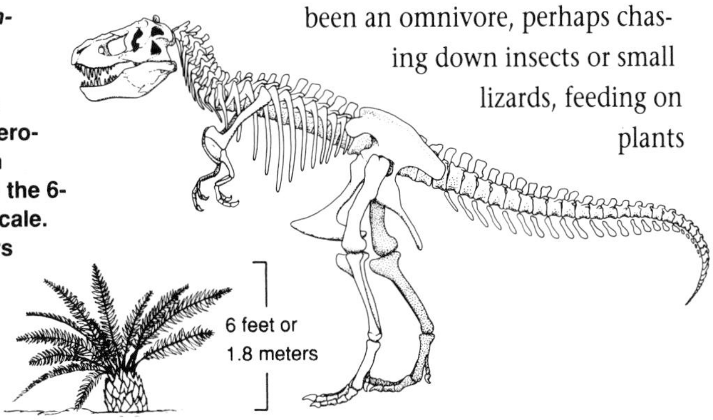

Figure 35. *Tyrannosaurus rex*, shown here in skeletal view, is typical of the theropod saurischian dinosaurs. Note the 6-foot cycad for scale. All the dinosaurs in this chapter are drawn to the same scale.

6 feet or 1.8 meters

good runners and small, ranging in size from 2 feet (60 centimeters) to around 12 feet (3.7 meters). Birds evolved from coelurosaurs some time during the Jurassic Period (193- to 136-million years ago). Many researchers feel that this group of dinosaurs were the most intelligent of the dinosaurs because in relation to the body size, the brain cavity was the largest of any of the dinosaurs. Some members of this infraorder possessed an almost opposable finger which could be used to aid in grasping objects.

Colorado has the distinction of having the first specimen of one of the coelurosaurid dinosaurs, This dinosaur, *Ornithomimus*, was discovered in the Cretaceous portion of the Denver Formation west of Denver in 1889. The name *Ornithomimus* means "bird mimic" which pretty well describes this dinosaur. *Ornithomimus* was a speedy long-legged dinosaur which looked much like an ostrich. Like ostriches and other birds, its head was relatively small and the mouth was devoid of teeth. Unlike birds it possessed a long tail which served as a counterbalance as it ran. It reached a size of 11.5 feet (3.5 meters). This dinosaur may have been an omnivore, perhaps chasing down insects or small lizards, feeding on plants

with the help of its grasping hands, or even feeding on the eggs of other dinosaurs.

Other saurischian dinosaurs may be loosely grouped into a large contingent called the carnosaurs (flesh lizards). As the name implies, here are the predators of the dinosaur world. Dinosaurs of this group are many and varied, but all made their living by eating meat. They include the mighty *Tyrannosaurus rex* (39 feet or 12 meters in length and 18.5 feet or 5.6 meters tall, Figure 32) and many small, but lethal predators, such as *Deinonychus* which reached a length of 8 to 13 feet (2.4 to 4 meters). These smaller predators may have hunted in packs like wolves of today. There may be as many as nine different families of carnosaurs. Many different types of carnivorous dinosaurs have been found in Colorado and are discussed in Chapters 6 and 7 of this book.

Ornithischian or Bird-Hipped Dinosaurs

Ornithischian, or bird-hipped dinosaurs, make up the other inhabitants of the dinosaur world. Like sauropods, ornithischians were herbivores. The similarity ends here for ornithischian dinosaurs are a wide variety of different types of dinosaurs which are most commonly found in Cretaceous rocks. Some ran fleetly on two legs while others lumbered over the landscape on all four. Still others possessed bony body armor or plates extending along their backbone. Some even had strangely ornamented skulls while others sprouted a variety of formidable horns on their skull. Most ornithischians also possessed a toothless horny beak, much like a bird.

Characteristics seen in the skeletons of the ornithischians allow them to be divided into three smaller groups (Figure 32). The largest group of ornithischians are the ornithopods (bird foot) with perhaps seven families. They are followed by the ceratopsians (horned face) and pachycephalosaurs (literally the thick headed, or bone headed) with possibly four families and the ankylosaurids (armored lizards) and stegosaurids (plated lizard) which contain four families. Representatives of all these major groups have been found in Colorado.

Ornithopods

Ornithopods, the "bird-foot" dinosaurs are the largest group of ornithischian dinosaurs (Figure 36). Although many of the these dinosaurs do not possess a "bird-like" foot, they have many characteristics in common. They appeared in the Late Triassic as small bipedal herbivores with teeth along the sides and in front of the jaw. This large group of dinosaurs did not flourish until the Cretaceous Period of the Mesozoic Era. Early in their history these dinosaurs were the only group of ornithischians which, when the need arose, could run around on their hind legs. In order to help their bipedal stance, many ornithopods rigidly held their tails parallel to the ground. A trellis-like series of bony tendons along the backbone

strengthened it, allowing the tail to be carried erect. The erect tail acted to counterbalance the weight of the fore part of the body.

Teeth of the early ornithopods were in different shapes and sizes, like mammals of today. By the Cretaceous, many of these dinosaurs had lost not only the differentiated dentition, but also the teeth in front of the mouth. Front teeth were replaced by a horny bird-like beak that allowed them to efficiently crop the tough Cretaceous vegetation. Teeth on the sides of the mouth became altered to row upon row of identical teeth that formed an efficient grinding mill or scissors-like pathway that cut and crushed the tough vegetation.

Most ornithopods moved around on three-toed feet with the toes terminating in hooves rather than claws, especially in the larger forms which reached the size of an elephant. Other ornithopods, especially the early ones, never reached the size of an elephant, they were fleet footed herbivores which were the size of a dog. This entire group of dinosaurs filled an ecologic niche that today is occupied by the gazelles, cervids (the deer family) and water buffalo.

Ceratopsians

Ornithischians with ornamented skulls comprise a second group of related dinosaurs. Some members, the ceratopsians, sprouted facial horns like our present day rhinoceros while others, the pachycephalosaurs, developed thick ornamented skulls. These modifications of the bones of the skull may have been for defense and/or shows of dominance.

Ceratopsians are usually distinguished by their well developed parrot-like hooked beak, one or more horns on the face and a bony frill which extends backwards from the back and sides of the skull (Figure 37). Most ceratopsians traveled over the landscape on all fours. The abundance of fossils of the horned ceratopsians indicates that they may have journeyed over the landscape in large herds. Ceratopsians were one of the last dinosaurs to evolve, appearing right around the Jurassic-Cretaceous boundary (136-million years ago). About 85-million years ago many different types evolved. All of the various forms looked alike from the neck back to the tail. However, when viewed face on the varieties became easily apparent. Some ceratopsians possessed only a nose horn,

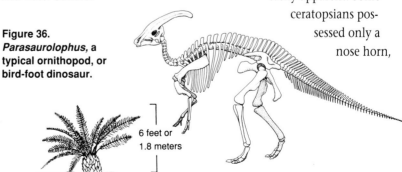

Figure 36.
***Parasaurolophus*, a typical ornithopod, or bird-foot dinosaur.**

6 feet or 1.8 meters

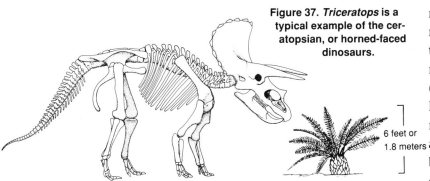

Figure 37. *Triceratops* is a typical example of the ceratopsian, or horned-faced dinosaurs.

6 feet or 1.8 meters

some had three horns and others had as many as seven horns or spines projecting from the skull and bony frill which extended backwards over the neck area.

Needless to say there are some exceptions to the rules. *Psittacosaurus* (parrot reptile) was an early ceratopsian that did not possess horns (a frill), had clawed hands, and was even bipedal. Its tie to the ceratopsians is the arrangement of the bones in the upper jaw which in life were covered with a horny beak. Psittacosaurs have been found in association with another different member of the ceratopsian clan, *Protoceratops* (before horned face), a dinosaur made famous not so much for itself, but for the fact that fossil bones of these dinosaurs were in association with nests full of eggs. *Protoceratops* has all of the characteristics of the suborder except for the lack of a horn.

Pachycephalosaurs, the bone-headed dinosaurs, are included in this group of ornithischians because the structure of the bones in the skull is similar to that seen in ceratopsians. Not much was known about this family of dinosaurs until

recently when the massive bony skulls were finally found in association with postcranial bones of the skeleton. These dinosaurs were bipedal and may have used their heads as battering rams in fights for dominance within their herd. Cretaceous rocks in Colorado have yielded the skull of one of the pachycephalosaurs.

Ankylosaurids and Stegosaurids
Lumbering armored dinosaurs make up another style of ornithischians called ankylosaurids (fused or joined together reptiles) and stegosaurids (the roof lizards or plated dinosaurs). All of these ornithischians were quadrupedal and possessed various types of body armor, including bony plates and nodules, spikes and/or bony clubs on the ends of their tails (Figure 38 and 39). They

Figure 38. *Euoplocephalus*, a typical ankylosaurid or armored dinosaur. Note the cycads for scale. Cycads were one food source of herbivorous dinosaurs throughout the Mesozoic Era.

6 feet or 1.8 meters

ranged in size from about 6 feet (1.8 meters) in length and about 1.5-feet tall (.5 meters) to over 35 feet (10.7 meters) in length and over 6-feet (1.8-meters) tall. Although ankylosaurids appear early in the fossil record (during the Early Jurassic, about 190-million years ago), their best success was during the Cretaceous Period (136- to 65-million years ago). During the summer of 1990 several dermal scutes, or bones which in life were imbedded in the skin as armor, were found in the Jurassic rocks of the Morrison Formation in western Colorado.

Bony plates may have had more than a protective function in dinosaurs. In stegosaurs these plates projected outward along the back and may have been used to regulate body temperature. Even though most elementary age children are quick to identify a stegosaurid, little is really known about this group. They appear in the fossil record during the Jurassic (Figure 32). They evolved rapidly and by the Late Jurassic many different types of stegosaurs were present. They began to decline quickly both in numbers and variety around the boundary between the Jurassic and Cretaceous (Figure 32). All of the stegosaurs became extinct sometime during the Cretaceous prior to the extinction of all of the dinosaurs.

All stegosaurids wandered the landscape on all fours, although they may have been able to rear up on their hind legs to browse in the trees. Two types existed, one with plates along the back and the other with mostly spikes along the tail and lower part of the back. In relation to the body, the head was fairly small and members of this group are noted for their relatively small-brain size. An enlarged area along the spinal cord in the pelvis of the stegosaurs probably helped to control the motor coordination of these animals. Their small slender head contained many small specialized leaf-shaped teeth along the margins of the jaw. A small bird-like beak completed the food processing apparatus in this herbivore.

Stegosaurids ranged in size from about 8 feet (2.4 meters) to nearly 25 feet (7.6 meters) in length. *Stegosaurus* is the best known genus and is the largest in size.

Although the first stegosaurids were discovered and described by the famous English naturalist Sir Richard Owen in 1875, the partial skeleton he described was surpassed by the discovery of the genus *Stegosaurus* in Colorado by Edward Cope and Othniel Marsh. Not only were these specimens larger than the English find, but the skeletons were more complete.

Many theories still abound as to the function of the plates which projected outward along the back of the stegosaurids. Although researchers agree that the bony spikes which projected from the tip of the tail were for defense, they still can not agree as to the exact function of the plates, on how many plates there were, or how they were arranged along the backbone. Part of the reason for this is

that the bony almost triangular shaped plates did not articulate with any other bone in the body. Even in the best preserved specimens, the plates are separated from the backbone so the arrangement in life and the total number can only be an educated guess.

All of the plates have a very rough surface which upon closer examination is a surface marked with many long and sometimes sinuous grooves and circular holes. These features were once the pathways of the many arteries and veins that were part of the stegosaur's circulatory system. Because these plates were covered with veins and arteries it can be deduced that in life the plates were covered with skin. Many researchers argue that the presence of such large numbers of veins and arteries leads to the conclusion that the plates served as heat regulators. If the stegosaur was trying to warm its body it could stand with its plates facing the sun in order to absorb the radiant heat. If the stegosaur was too warm it could stand at right angles to the sun, thus exposing less area to the sun's warming effect. In effect these plates acted like a radiator, absorbing or dissipating heat depending on the needs of the animal.

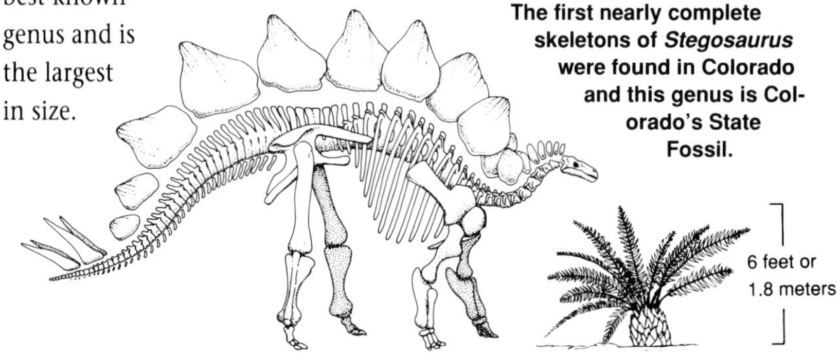

Figure 39. *Stegosaurus*, a typical stegosaurid, or plated dinosaur. The first nearly complete skeletons of *Stegosaurus* were found in Colorado and this genus is Colorado's State Fossil.

6 feet or 1.8 meters

THE DAWN OF COLORADO'S DINOSAURS, A TIME OF TROPICAL LATITUDES AND ARID LOWLANDS

TODAY VISITORS WILL TRAVEL through many different ecological zones as they trace historical discoveries and current research related to dinosaurs throughout Colorado. In a few-hundred miles they will encounter the prairies of eastern Colorado, the alpine environment of the central peaks and the high desert of the western plateaus. During the reign of the dinosaurs such a rapid change from one environment to another was not nearly as common. At times the land was miles and miles of monotonous landscape which was near, at, or below sea level during the Mesozoic Era (225- to 65-million years ago). This and the next two chapters illustrate the general environments and the dinosaurs that existed in Colorado as they made their appearance around 205-million years ago

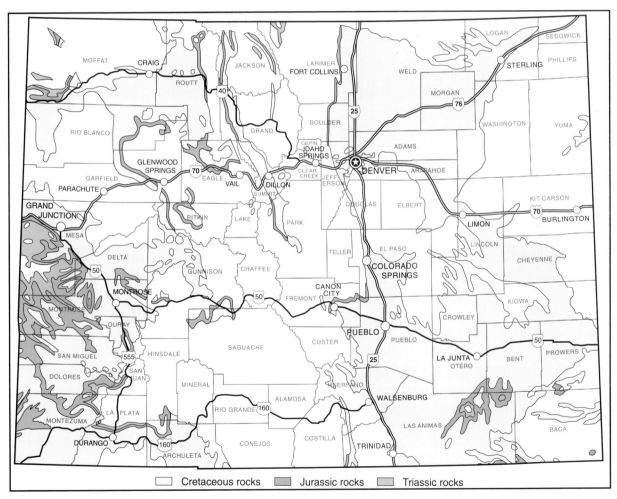

Figure 40. Rocks deposited during the Mesozoic Era in Colorado.

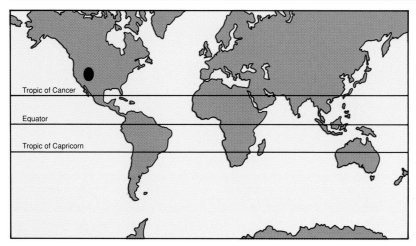

Figure 41. Location of the continents and oceans today. The black oval indicates the location of Colorado, Wyoming and Utah.

during the Triassic Period (225- to 193-million years ago), evolved to giants during the Jurassic Period (193- to 136-million years ago, Chapter 6) and next developed into a wide variety of types and forms before they became extinct at the end of the Cretaceous Period (136- to 65-million years ago, Chapter 7).

Colorado's tale of dinosaurs begins in the Late Triassic rocks of the state. Unfortunately both the sparse surface exposures (Figure 40) and the fossils found within these rocks raise more questions about Colorado's Triassic dinosaurs than answers revealed. Rough terrain also complicates the study of the state's Triassic rocks. Fortunately these rocks are better exposed in surrounding states and paleontologists can make good educated guesses as to Colorado's Triassic climate and dinosaurs. It is a story that will no doubt become clearer as these Triassic rocks are further studied.

Colorado's Late Triassic rocks were deposited on land in a semi-arid environment. Sediments that are deposited in this environment often take on a reddish color which is retained when these sediments lithify, or turn to stone. Geologists often refer to such rocks as redbeds. Rocks that were deposited around the time when dinosaurs evolved are called the Chinle Formation in Colorado (see Figure 22). The Chinle is a series of redbeds which record

the presence of vast ancient mud-flats upon which dinosaurs and other reptiles left their footprints. Interbedded with the fine grained sediments of the mudflats are discontinuous sandstones and limestones which were deposited in streams and lakes. Some of the sandstones record the presence of ancient sand dunes, often as light-tan or pinkish sandstones with massive angled bedding planes, or crossbeds. The streams and lakes filled during a wet season and dried out during hot and dry times. It is not known how long the wet and dry cycles lasted, only that they did exist. As the streams and lakes dried, they left vast areas of drying mud upon which mudcracks developed and early dinosaurs and other reptiles left tracks.

Finding evidence of ancient hot and cyclically dry conditions in Colorado may at first sound strange, but when the Late Triassic redbeds are

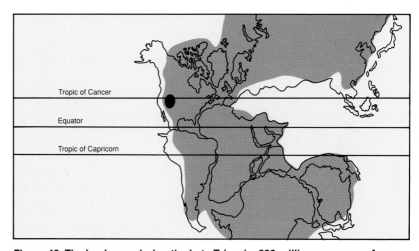

Figure 42. The landmass during the Late Triassic, 200-million years ago. Areas covered by water are blue and areas of land are brown. The black outlines are the continents as they look today but fitted together to form the land as it might have appeared then. Note that the states of Colorado, Wyoming and Utah (black oval) were well within tropical latitudes.

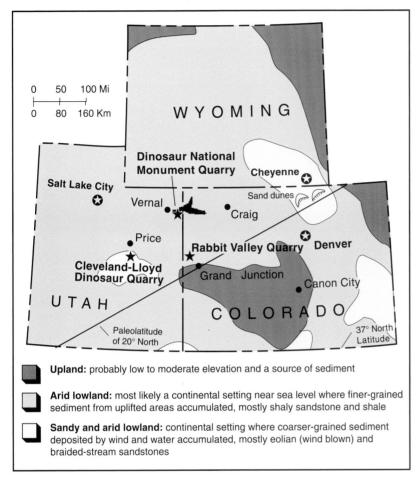

Figure 43. Late Triassic paleogeography present in Colorado, Wyoming and Utah as dinosaurs evolved and began to dominate the land fauna.

along the western side of a large landmass (Figure 42).

Using the present as a key to the past, today's geologists therefore expect to find evidence of arid environments in Colorado's Triassic rocks. This is indeed the case because the state's Triassic redbeds record the presence of ancient arid conditions, along with indications of wetter periods. Wetter periods are even seen today in the world's tropical to subtropical dry climates. A climate such as this is certainly not the typical environment that one would expect for the appearance of a group such as the dinosaurs which today are still often erroneously pictured as wallowing around in swamps surrounded by steaming tropical rain forests. This was a harsh environment but the footprints and a few body fossils found in the Triassic rocks of Colorado, Wyoming, and Utah indicate that life was abundant. Figure 43 shows the extent of this dry tropical to subtropical climate in these states. Note that the paleolatitude of 20-degrees north headed northeast through the Grand Junction, Colorado area.

The scene depicted in Figure 44 may have taken place during the Late Triassic in Colorado. A lone dinosaur (*Coelophysis*) runs across mudflats on the edge of a lake, leaving its footprints. Nearly complete skeletons of this early primitive dinosaur which was about the size of a grown person have been found at Ghost Ranch in northwestern New Mexico near the Colorado border. It is probable that these dinosaurs also

studied in the context of the ancient position of the continents it is easy to see how this happened. Dinosaurs made their appearance worldwide about 205-million years ago near the end of the Triassic Period. Due to the slow but relentless forces of continental drift, the continents had a completely different configuration during the Late Triassic (compare the present day continental configuration with the Late Triassic configuration in Figures 41 and 42). Colorado and her sister states of Wyoming and Utah were situated on the western

side of a large landmass in the tropical to subtropical latitudes that we see in today's world. (Note the black oval which represents Colorado, Wyoming, and Utah on Figures 41 and 42.) Today when continents fall within the tropics, prevailing winds often dry the western sides of the landmasses, creating dry desert like conditions. Today these areas contain the Sahara Desert or the Australian Outback. Note that during the Late Triassic as dinosaurs evolved, Colorado, Wyoming and Utah were located in the tropics

Figure 44. A scene that could have taken place in the Late Triassic in Colorado.

lived in Colorado. *Coelophysis* is typical of Triassic dinosaurs, all were fairly small and bipedal. Pictured with *Coelophysis* are two reptiles whose fossils are often found in Late Triassic redbeds of other states. Crocodile-like thecodont reptiles, phytosaurs, lounge on the sides of the lake while an armored herbivorous thecodont reptile, an aetosaur, wanders across the landscape. The crocodile-like phytosaurs were the main and largest predator of the Late

Triassic, reaching a length of up to 12 feet (3.6 meters). Teeth of these predators have been found in Colorado. In the right middle ground an aetosaur, one of the armored herbivorous thecodonts traverses the mudflat. Some isolated plates from its heavily armored body have been found in Colorado.

These animals and others, perhaps never to be known, did leave trace fossils at three documented sites, all on Colorado's Western

Slope. These sites, two located southwest of Grand Junction and one in the northwestern corner of Colorado record the coming and going of a variety of reptiles, even a dinosaur or two. With the present state of the art of interpreting footprints, it is still not possible to assign what specific animals may have made these tracks although the footprints can often be assigned to a certain family of animals.

DINOSAUR GIANTS FROM A VAST LOWLAND

ROCKS DEPOSITED DURING THE JURASSIC PERIOD, 193- to 136-million years ago record many changing environments in Colorado. Early in the Jurassic arid conditions were dominant and thick deposits of windblown sand accumulated—especially in the western part of Colorado and surrounding states. Following the arid period, a shallow sea invaded the western interior from the north. After the sea withdrew, about 155-million years ago, Colorado and adjacent areas were uplifted to expose a vast flat area crisscrossed by streams and dotted with lakes. This vast lowland covered many states (Figure 45). It was under these conditions that sediments of the world-famous Morrison Formation began to accumulate. Besides dinosaur fossils, the Morrison Formation is known for its uranium ore. Prospecting for uranium in the Morrison has led to the discovery of more than one dinosaur fossil locality. One of the most famous sites discovered during the heyday of uranium prospecting was the Dry Mesa Quarry near Delta, Colorado (refer to Chapter 2).

Because of the vast areal extent of the Morrison Formation, one might assume that this unit is rather monotonous and uniform throughout. However, one quick look at a typical exposure of the Morrison with its multi-colored mudstones and abrupt lithologic changes between mudstones, sandstones, and limestones will leave even the most experienced field geologist a little puzzled. These internal complexities

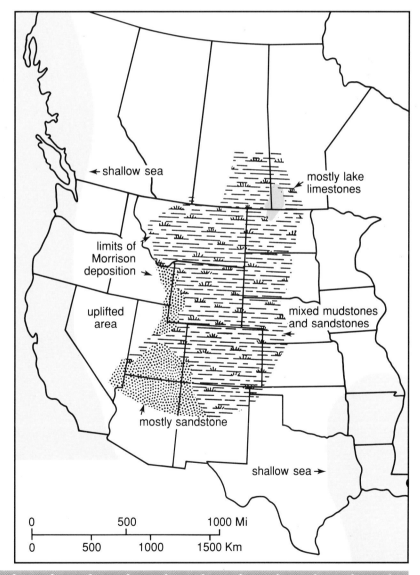

Figure 45. The original extent of the Morrison Formation along with areas of land or shallow seas.

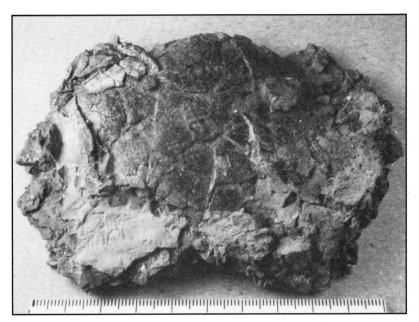

Figure 46. This crushed fossilized egg is the most complete one found in a fossilized nest discovered in the lower portion of the Morrison Formation on Colorado's Western Slope by geologist Dr. Robert Young and his students. The nest contained many other egg fragments and small bones, perhaps the baby reptiles and/or prey brought back to the nest by the adult nest makers.

are typical of sediments deposited in a continental setting where environments quickly change from upland area to stream valley, lake or floodplain. A look around Denver serves as a good example of how quickly these environments can change. Within a few short miles people can stand in the Platte River Valley in central Denver or on the foothills on the western edge of town. Imagine all of this buried and then trying to figure out what happened and you have a feel for the complexities of the Morrison Formation.

Rocks of the Morrison Formation started to accumulate around 155-million years ago and appears

to have stopped around 140-million years ago. Throughout Colorado the thickness and exact age of the Morrison rocks vary. However, these rocks do give geologists and paleontologists enough information to reconstruct a good picture of what life was like during the 15 million years when the Morrison Formation was deposited. This was a time when dinosaurs were many and varied, a time when giant herbivorous dinosaurs lived alongside car-

nivorous dinosaurs the size of a chicken. In addition to dinosaur bones, a fossilized nest complete with eggs (Figure 46) and traces of dinosaurs in the form of footprints and trackways have been discovered in the rocks of Colorado's Morrison Formation. Today there are dozens of sites within Colorado that either await excavation or are being studied by both amateur and professional dinosaur researchers.

As the Morrison Formation began to accumulate during the Late Jurassic, the forces of continental drift had rotated Colorado northward out of the tropics (Figure 47). This change in latitude brought a change in the environment. No longer were sand dunes and intermittent streams and lakes characteristic of an arid environment present. Instead this was a time that was per-

Figure 47. By the end of the deposition of the Morrison Formation around 140-million years ago, the continents, outlined as they look today, had drifted into the position shown above. By this time Colorado, Wyoming and Utah (black oval) were out of the tropical latitudes, but the climate was still warm. Areas covered by the oceans are blue and areas of land are brown.

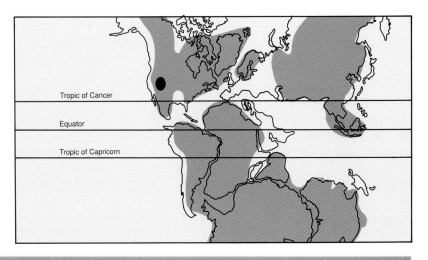

haps similar to the present dry savannas in Africa. The landscape was broad and fairly featureless, perhaps only broken by the presence of a lake or river (Figure 48). Large lakes occasionally dotted the landscape and rivers, both braided and meandering cut the monotony of the landscape (Figure 49). No doubt vegetation of the time, mostly towering ancestral gymnosperms (plants with naked seeds such as conifers) and smaller gymnosperms such as cycads, were most prevalent near these bodies of water. These areas attracted the dinosaurs of the Jurassic (see cover illustration).

However, an interpretation pried from the Morrison rocks indicates that life was not easy. Water levels in the bodies of water were subject to fluctuation because Colorado experienced a cyclic monsoon when winds changed direction and the landscape became scorched and dry. The duration of these cycles can not be determined. This desiccation of the landscape occurred repeatedly. As the bodies of water began to shrink as they dried, vegetation no doubt withered on the drying landscape. Herbivorous dinosaurs were forced to migrate in their search for food, perhaps miles away.

Large sauropods, which were common during this time, probably wandered from one body of water to another, constantly in search of new water holes with their borders of vegetation. Predators such as *Allosaurus, Ceratosaurus and Epanterias* may have followed the herds, constantly on the watch for young, sick or aged sauropods who were struggling to survive the migration

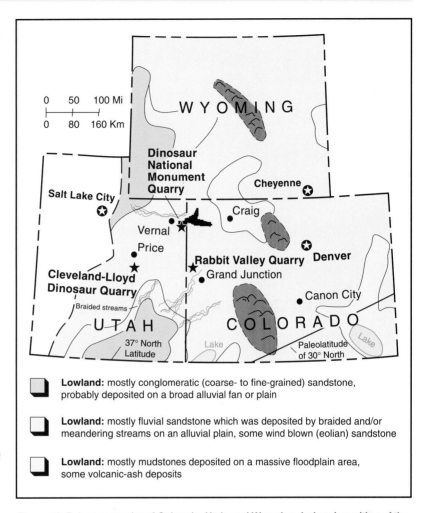

Figure 48. Paleogeography of Colorado, Utah, and Wyoming during deposition of the Morrison Formation, 155- to 140-million years ago. During the days of the dinosaur giants of the Jurassic, the environment was fairly uniform throughout this area.

to a more lush area. In Figure 49, in the upper left of the illustration, a group of brachiosaurids migrates along the shoreline of a large playa lake while a lone diplodocid fords a stream which empties into the lake (right center). Carnivores of the day, *Allosaurus* (lower left) and *Cerato- saurus* (center) prowl the stream inhabited by crocodiles, perhaps in search of easy scavenging of a dinosaur that may have died and has been washed downstream. On

the lower right, *Stegosaurus* keeps a wary eye on the predators near the site of a nest.

Dinosaurs from the Morrison Formation have made Colorado famous. No other rock formation in Colorado has yielded such an abundance and diversity of dinosaurs as the Morrison. Some of the world's largest and smallest dinosaurs have been discovered in these rocks (Figure 50). It is easy to see why the Jurassic Period is often referred to as the time of giant dinosaurs. Unlike the preceding Triassic and the succeeding Cretaceous Period, most of the dinosaurs were larger than a man.

Mesa County, Colorado holds the distinction of having three of the four largest dinosaurs currently known. Although the skeletons of these three were not complete, researchers were able to assign them to the second, third and fourth place in size for worldwide discoveries. The most complete skeleton found was *Brachiosaurus altithorax*, a large herbivorous sauropod found by Elmer Riggs during his turn of the century excavations just

west of Grand Junction. The genus *Brachiosaurus* ranged in size from 75 to 90 feet (22.8 to 27.4 meters) and his height came in around 40 feet (12.2 meters). These dinosaurs actually held the record as the world's largest until 1972 when a huge 8-foot- (2.4 meters) long shoulder blade was discovered at the Dry Mesa Quarry near Delta, Colorado. More of the skeleton was subsequently discovered and described years later. Paleontologists called this giant *Supersaurus*. From projections based on measurements of the bones, this dinosaur may have ranged in length from 80 to 100 feet (24.2 to 30.5 meters). It may have been 54 feet (16.5

meters) in height. *Supersaurus* was one of the diplodocids, sauropods with a long whip-like tail, slender body and large size. Recently more bones possibly of this same genus have been unearthed at the Mygatt-Moore Dinosaur Quarry (see Chapter 8) near the Colorado-Utah border.

Supersaurus retained the title of the world's largest dinosaur until 1979 when an even larger dinosaur was discovered, again at Dry Mesa Quarry. A single vertebra from the backbone was unearthed and dubbed *"Ultrasaurus"* by the paleontologists. Subsequently a tail vertebra, a neck vertebra and a shoulder blade were interpreted as

Figure 49. A typical life scene in Colorado from around 155- to 140-million years ago during the deposition of the Jurassic Morrison Formation.

being from this new giant dinosaur. These bones most closely resemble bones of a brachiosaurid, a sauropod characterized by its thick heavy body, stout tail and long neck. This new genus of dinosaur has not yet been accepted by the scientific community as a valid genus so its name has quotes around it. It has been interpreted that this beast was at least 100 feet (30.5 meters) long.

Other large sauropod bones have been found at the Dry Mesa Quarry, but there is a problem because the bones were disarticulated, making it difficult to reconstruct a skeleton. Perhaps future excavations at this site will shed light on these tantalizing glimpses of giant dinosaurs from the Morrison Formation. For the moment these giants from Mesa County hold the distinction of being second (*Ultrasaurus*), third (*Supersaurus*) and fourth (*Brachiosaurus*) in size. They are currently eclipsed by the giant *Seismosaurus,* another Jurassic sauropod discovered in 1979 by hikers in northwestern New Mexico near the town of Cuba. Presently the skeleton is being excavated, prepared and described.

Some paleontologists have long been interested in small dinosaurs or other animals which lived alongside the dinosaur giants of the Jurassic. The collecting technique used by researchers usually yields a wealth of small animal fossils. These smaller fossils, which paleontologists call microvertebrates, are more economical to collect than large dinosaurs. Sometimes these small fossils lead to a better interpretation of the ancient climate because smaller animals do not

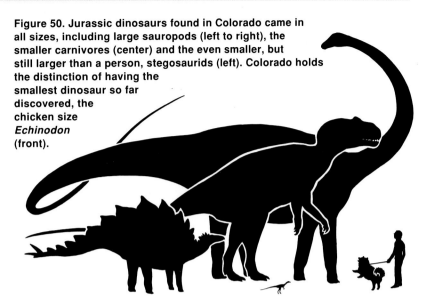

Figure 50. Jurassic dinosaurs found in Colorado came in all sizes, including large sauropods (left to right), the smaller carnivores (center) and the even smaller, but still larger than a person, stegosaurids (left). Colorado holds the distinction of having the smallest dinosaur so far discovered, the chicken size *Echinodon* (front).

migrate for long distances across different ecological zones. A good example is west of Grand Junction at a locality called the Fruita Paleontological Area. At this site the discovery of fossilized bones of small amphibians corroborates the presence of permanent water in the form of a stream that ran through the area. In the past a few fossils of the smaller animals of the Late Jurassic were collected in Garden Park near Canon City. However, early expeditions in Colorado were more interested in the hunt for large dinosaurs.

Study of the small animals of the Morrison has yielded interesting discoveries, including a dinosaur the size of a chicken. This little dinosaur, *Echinodon,* is described in the *Guinness Book of World Records* as the world's smallest dinosaur. *Echinodon* was a herbivorous ornithischian dinosaur related to the ornithopods which were dominant in the Cretaceous. The Fruita Paleontological Area specimen, which still awaits scientific

description, was previously known only from Europe. Like today's chicken, *Echinodon* was bipedal with the hind legs longer than the front limbs (refer to Figure 50). This little dinosaur measured 20 inches (50 centimeters) from its snout to the end of its tail. The discovery of this dinosaur was another first for Mesa County, Colorado and puts the county on the map for having some of the largest and smallest dinosaurs discovered.

Many other small animals and plants have been found within the rocks of the Morrison Formation at the Fruita Paleontological Area. Another bipedal dinosaur, a carnivore with affinities to the coelurosaurids (dinosaurs with hollow bones like today's birds), has been found. Many other types of reptiles, including crocodilians, turtles, cousins of present day lizards, and a new type of snake have been discovered by slow and meticulous digging in the Morrison. Some of these reptiles were carnivores and some were herbivores. Even amphibian and fish fossils have been extracted from the rocks. A wide variety of early mammals, all about the size of today's rodents have been unearthed. Many of these are new primitive types and once they are formally described they should add much to the knowledge of the small primitive mammals that hid in the vegetation while the dinosaur giants roamed the land.

Some of the invertebrate fossils found at the site help in interpreting the environment of the immediate area and give hints of what was happening on a broader scale during deposition of the Morrison. Freshwater clams found are indicative of permanent water. Crayfish, both the animals and their burrows, and snails have turned up. These animals love semiaquatic conditions, thus it is interpreted that dry land was nearby. This interpretation is corroborated by the abundance of terrestrial reptiles and mammals fossils found at the site.

Fossilized wood from Jurassic gymnosperms documents the presence of large trees on the landscape. On an exceedingly smaller scale, microscopic fossils obtained from pulverized rocks of the Morrison Formation have been identified as spores and pollen from long dead trees and shrubs that lived during the Jurassic. These microscopic plant fossils indicate the climate was relatively dry. Gathering all of the evidence from the large variety of animals and plants indicates that during deposition of the Morrison a fairly large and complex land ecosystem was present. Perhaps the vegetation and small ani-

mals were confined to areas near permanent water while large dinosaurs were free to roam from one vegetated area to another. An environment very similar to this exists on the savannas of present day Africa.

Rocks of the Morrison Formation confirm the savanna scenario and add further details about the paleogeography. A close study of the rocks leads to an interpretation that there were times when mountain building processes, including volcanoes, were active in western Utah. Erupting volcanoes at times added a large amount of volcanic ash to the ecosystem. Clouds of ash larger than those from the 1980 eruption of Mount St. Helens in Washington state may have killed off numerous dinosaurs. Many dinosaur bones have been discovered in these layered beds of weathered volcanic ash. Evidence of this ancient volcanism is preserved as layers of bentonite, an expandable clay that is composed of weathered volcanic ash. Bentonite can be dated because it contains small amounts of radioactive particles. Dates obtained from bentonite help assign ages to rocks which were deposited during different geologic periods.

As geologists studied rocks of the Morrison Formation, they found evidence that the climate fluctuated between wet and dry conditions as the Morrison Formation accumulated. Fluvial (river deposited) sandstones suggest that permanent water was present; limestone layers show that the landscape became parched and dry. As the ephemeral lakes began to dry, the lake waters became supersaturated with calcium

carbonate dissolved in the water, and limestone began to precipitate.

On Colorado's Western Slope, rocks of the Morrison Formation have recently yielded other secrets related to the ancient life of the area. In the lower part of the Morrison of Delta County, Colorado, Dr. Robert Young, a consulting geologist from Grand Junction, has discovered what is currently the oldest known fossilized nest in North America complete with eggs and other fossils. Dr. Young's discovery was made while he and two Egyptian geologists were measuring thicknesses of the rocks in the lower part of the Morrison Formation. Regional correlations with other Jurassic rocks that have been dated suggest this nest may be 153- to 155-million years old. Successive layering of the rocks in the nest indicates that it was probably occupied a number of times. Many different microfossils of animals and plants have been found. Fragments of teeth and bones from a variety of animals suggest that the nest was probably that of a carnivorous reptile which may have brought prey back to its young. The tiny plant fossils, including seeds and wood, may indicate that plant material was used in the construction of the nest or was used to cover the eggs to help keep them warm.

In the southeastern corner of Colorado abundant dinosaur trace fossils, in the form of tracks and trackways, offer clues about the behavior of dinosaurs. Fairly large lakes developed on the land at the time of the Morrison deposition. At the site (Figure 51) over 1,300 individual footprints show that sauropods were traveling subparallel to one another in a herd, probably along the shore of a large lake. It has also been interpreted that the dinosaur fauna of the time was dominated by the large sauropods and theropods, an interpretation which is supported by the body fossils of these animals found in the Morrison Formation at other Colorado sites and in adjoining states.

One episode which Colorado's Jurassic age rocks do not record is large extinction of dinosaurs which occurred at the boundary between the Jurassic and Cretaceous. In Colorado the boundary between the Jurassic and the Cretaceous rocks is marked by an extensive unconformity, or lack of a continuous record. There may be as much as 15-million years missing from the rock record (refer to Figure 22). Perhaps somewhere near the top of the Morrison

Formation a clue may yet be found as to why many of the large sauropods, the stegosaurs and the typical Jurassic carnivores like *Allosaurus* and *Ceratosaurus* suddenly became extinct, to be replaced by many new and varied types of dinosaurs. Although many new types of dinosaurs evolved during the Cretaceous Period, none of these new dinosaurs ever grew as large as the giant sauropods from Colorado's Morrison Formation.

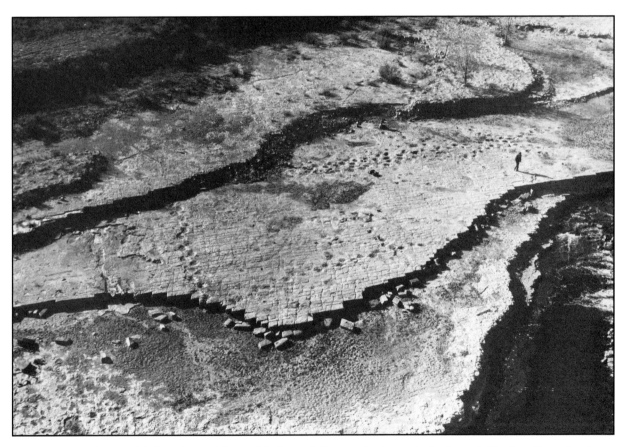

Figure 51. An oblique aerial view of one of the world's-longest dinosaur trackways in the Jurassic Morrison Formation in southeast Colorado along the Purgatoire River. This site contains hundreds of individual footprints and trackways made by both saurischian and ornithischian dinosaurs as they moved along what may have been the shore of an ancient large lake.

C H A P T E R   7

THE END OF AN ERA: THE SEA COMES AND GOES AS DINOSAURS LEAVE THE SCENE

URING THE CRETACEOUS many new types of dinosaurs evolved to fill the ecological niches left by the extinction of most of the Jurassic sauropods, stegosaurs and carnivores. Other types of dinosaurs evolved to fill new niches appearing on an ever changing landscape. During the Cretaceous this changing landscape was marked by the major invasion of a shallow sea, which advanced across Colorado from both the north and the south, eventually connecting the Gulf of Mexico with the Arctic Ocean (Figure 52). This transgression of the sea got a sporadic start about 125- to 120-million years ago and then rapidly began to invade the state around 110-million years ago. From 110-million years ago until the end of the Cretaceous at 65-million years ago sea level fluctuated greatly. Throughout most of this timespan much and sometimes all of Colorado was below sea level and rocks were deposited in this marine environment.

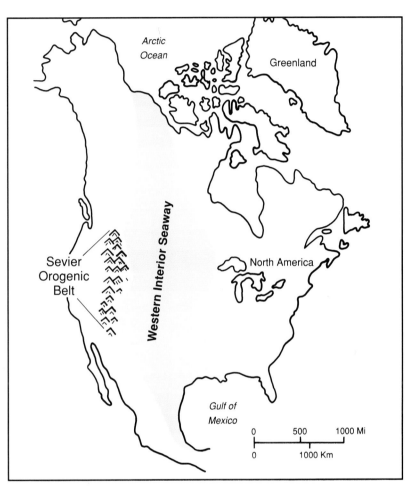

Figure 52. Extent of the Cretaceous seaway around 100-million years ago. The Sevier Orogenic Belt is an old mountain range that formed prior to the present-day Rocky Mountains.

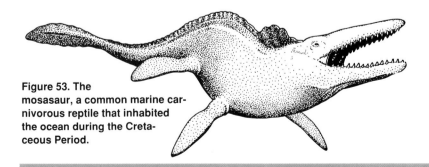

Figure 53. The mosasaur, a common marine carnivorous reptile that inhabited the ocean during the Cretaceous Period.

Because dinosaurs did not live in the marine environment, most of Colorado's Cretaceous age rocks do not contain any dinosaur fossils—although there is one noteworthy exception discussed later in this chapter. The marine deposits do record the presence of mosasaurs

45

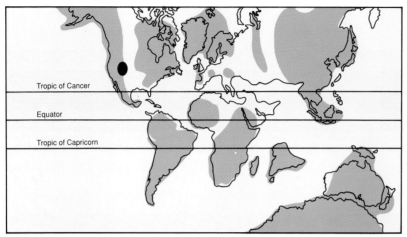

Figure 54. Current continental outlines configured as they were 100-million years ago, 10-million years after a shallow marine sea began to invade the State of Colorado. By this time, the seaway had reached its maximum extent. Areas in blue indicate water and brown indicates landmasses.

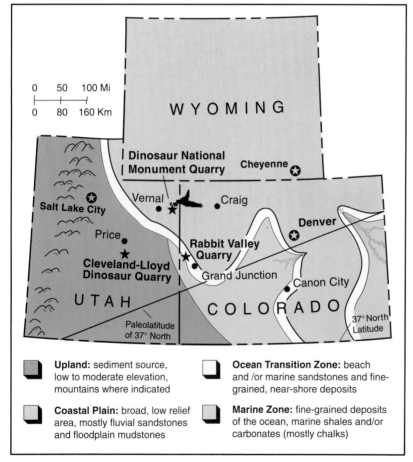

Figure 55. Around 110-million years ago a shallow sea began to flood Colorado. Dinosaurs inhabited a variety of environments from uplands to shorelines. Rocks deposited at this time contain dinosaur footprints.

(Figure 53) and plesiosaurs, large marine reptiles which inhabited the sea while dinosaurs roamed the land. Fossils of these extinct marine vertebrates have been found in Cretaceous rocks of the eastern foothills and plains and the Western Slope of the state.

By the time the seaway invaded Colorado, the continents, driven by the relentless forces of plate tectonics, began to take on an arrangement more like today (compare Figure 54 with Figure 41). Even though Colorado was well out of the tropical latitudes during the Cretaceous, the climate, as reconstructed from fossil evidence, was mild with a lack of any pronounced seasons. The presence of an inland sea helped in keeping the climate moist so cyclic dry spells seen in the Jurassic did not occur in the Cretaceous. This mild and moist climate resulted in lush rain forests being developed wherever the land poked above the surface of the sea within Colorado, Wyoming and Utah. Remains of these lush forests are preserved in thick coal deposits in western and eastern Colorado.

As the encroaching seaway first flooded Colorado in the Early Cretaceous and then receded as mountain building in Utah uplifted the landscape, many new and different environments were brought to the state. Around 110-million years ago a sinuous system of beaches wound their way through Colorado as the sea started to cover the old Jurassic landscape (Figure 55). Dinosaurs, perhaps searching for a certain food

Figure 56. As iguanodontid dinosaurs warily look over their shoulders at a carnivore on the other side of a tidal channel, primitive birds soar over plesiosaurs prowling a shallow sea just east of Denver nearly 110-million years ago.

source or migrating in response to slight seasonal variations in the climate, traversed these ribbons of sand as they traveled along the open beaches rather than the heavily forested landscape behind the beaches (Figure 56). No doubt these beaches were the path of least resistance to the dinosaurs. The scene depicted in Figure 56 may have taken place west of Denver near Red Rocks Park, for its is here that many dinosaur footprints can be seen in the now uplifted rocks. As this drawing shows, about 110-million years ago these rocks were a sandy beach, complete with a tidal channel which separates the her-

bivorous iguanodontids from a carnivorous theropod.

Within 10 million years the scene in Colorado changed dramatically, for by that time the sea had completely flooded Colorado. The beach which had been near Denver now ran north to south through central Utah (Figure 57), a westward migration of over 400 miles. In western Colorado a dinosaur fossil has been found in dark-gray to almost-black marine shales, which were deposited on the ocean floor when the sea was near its maximum transgression of Colorado, Wyoming, and Utah. It is extremely rare to find such a fossil

in the marine environment. As has happened in the past, amateurs were responsible for the initial discovery which was later excavated by a museum crew from the Museum of Western Colorado in Grand Junction. Researchers from the museum are elated because the fossil, a juvenile hadrosaur (duckbill), is a nearly complete skeleton representing one of the first finds of a dinosaur from this part of the Cretaceous. Paleontologists from the museum are currently trying to identify which specific hadrosaur they have recovered. Nearby, the remains of both a mosasaur and a plesiosaur were found. Both of

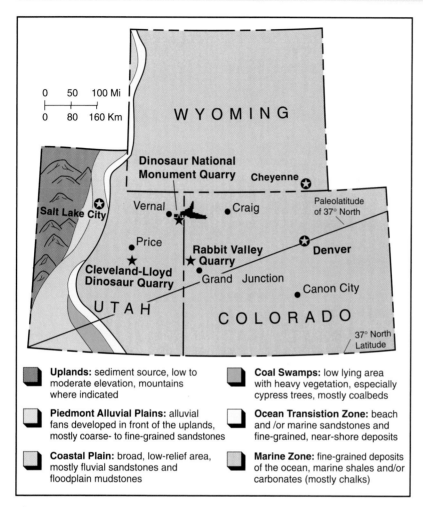

Uplands: sediment source, low to moderate elevation, mountains where indicated

Piedmont Alluvial Plains: alluvial fans developed in front of the uplands, mostly coarse- to fine-grained sandstones

Coastal Plain: broad, low-relief area, mostly fluvial sandstones and floodplain mudstones

Coal Swamps: low lying area with heavy vegetation, especially cypress trees, mostly coalbeds

Ocean Transistion Zone: beach and /or marine sandstones and fine-grained, near-shore deposits

Marine Zone: fine-grained deposits of the ocean, marine shales and/or carbonates (mostly chalks)

Figure 57. By 100-million years ago Colorado was completely flooded by a seaway. Dinosaurs followed the shoreline westward into Utah.

these marine reptiles were fairly common inhabitants of the Cretaceous sea. The rocks and the fossils from this site indicate that the body of the young hadrosaur may have been washed out to sea as much as 50 or 60 miles before it sank and came to rest on the ocean floor.

Colorado's Western Slope may have the only dinosaur in marine shales, but mosasaur and plesiosaur skeletons have also been found in the extensive Cretaceous age deposits which occur on Colorado's eastern plains (refer to Figure 21). Near Colorado Springs a fairly complete mosasaur was collected. In southern Colorado a nearly complete plesiosaur was found and now is on display at the Denver Museum of Natural History as is a mosasaur. To this day, local amateur paleontologists still occasionally discover a mosasaur tooth or bone as they explore the Cretaceous marine deposits east of the Front Range.

Like the age old saying of what goes up must come down, the rising sea level which flooded Colorado in the Early Cretaceous, began to fall in the Late Cretaceous. By 80-million years ago, as mountain building processes gathered steam in western Utah and started to uplift the land, the beaches were pushed back to the east, passing once again through Colorado, this time east of Craig in the western portion of the state and west of Canon City in central Colorado (Figure 58). During this time vast coals swamps formed in western and eastern Colorado. This period of time marked the beginning of the end of the last seaway and its deposits in Colorado.

With land once more exposed above sea level, dinosaurs followed the retreating shoreline and left fossils attesting to their presence. As in the early Cretaceous, fossils of these later Cretaceous dinosaurs are predominantly trace fossils, again in the form of footprints. These dinosaurs were not on the beach, but in the low areas farther back (Figure 59). This lowland was riddled with coal swamps which the dinosaurs used as a feeding ground. Many of the underground coal mines in western Colorado have footprints in the roofs of the mines, made millions of years ago as herbivorous dinosaurs, probably hadrosaurs, moved into the drying coal swamps to feed. Figure 59 illustrates what conditions were probably like. Note that the hadrosaurs are feeding on the edge of the water-logged portion of the coal swamp. The association of coal and dinosaur fossils (trace fossils in Colorado and trace and body fossils in other states) led many earlier researchers to the interpretation that dinosaurs lived in the swamp. However, geologists who specialize in interpreting ancient environments have pointed out that the footprints were made in rock units associated with either drying or development of a swamp. Thus the dinosaurs were moving into the drying or forming swamps to feed,

they were not actually living in the swamps. The footprints themselves support this conclusion for they often show that dinosaurs were standing with their hind toes pointed toward the coalified tree stumps, a good stance for feeding. Work by other dinosaur researchers, most notably Jack Horner in Montana, has shown that the hadrosaurs preferred drier ground for their nest sites.

Despite an abundance of footprints, very few body fossils of

dinosaurs have been discovered in these 80-million year old Cretaceous deposits. To date only a partial skeleton of a hadrosaur has been reported. This may be an enticing preview of what these mostly unexplored Cretaceous rocks contain for present and future explorers. The environment in which these Cretaceous rocks were deposited was perfect for fossilization, and many small vertebrate fossils, especially mammals, have been found within these rocks.

In terms of geologic time, the retreat of the sea was rapid, taking only about 10-million years. Dinosaurs easily kept pace, and by 70-million years ago they once again had all of Colorado as their homeland. Near the end of the Cretaceous, uplift of the Rocky Mountains had elevated Colorado to the point where the seaway was completely driven from the state (Figure 60). Gone was the sea but not so the lush vegetation. Although the coal swamps associated with the near marine environment had disappeared along with the sea, dinosaurs of the Late Cretaceous still had a relatively delectable choice of plants to feed upon. The topography was now beginning to show the influence of the mountain building episode which would produce the present day Rocky Mountains in a few-million years. Areas which were once vast low flatlands dotted with coal swamps now became gently rolling hills.

Shortly before the end of the Cretaceous Period a large variety of dinosaurs inhabited the land near

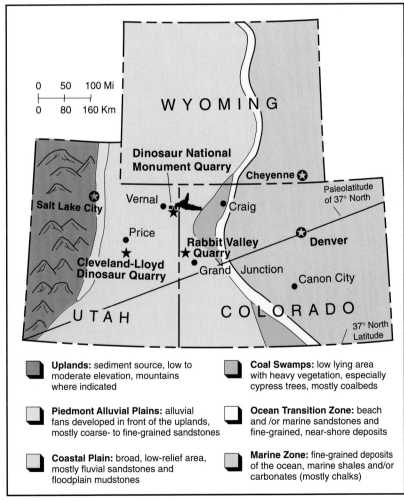

Figure 58. By 80-million years ago, during the Cretaceous Period, mountain building began to change the face of the landscape.

Figure 59. Dinosaurs, like these hadrosaurs (duckbills) fed on the edge of vast coal swamps that were present in western and eastern Colorado around 80-million years ago.

what is now Denver, Colorado. The fauna was dominated by the horned dinosaurs like Triceratops pictured in Figure 61 in the lower right corner. Bird-mimic dinosaurs (left center), armored dinosaurs (lower left), hadrosaurs, (upper left) and carnivorous dinosaurs (upper center) completed the dinosaur fauna. Small mammals (lower left) were soon to become an important part of fauna after the dinosaurs became extinct.

Dinosaurs which lived on this Late Cretaceous landscape were many and varied. One of the most common dinosaurs was the ceratopsian or horned dinosaur. Some

researchers think they may have been as plentiful as bison in the American West. As was discussed in Chapter 2, the Denver Formation immediately west of Denver yielded the first fossil of the ceratopsians.

Fleet-footed bird-mimic dinosaurs (ornithomimosaurs) also traversed the rolling landscape of the Late Cretaceous (Figure 61). The discovery in 1889 of a partial foot of this dinosaur was another first for Colorado, for it marked the discovery of a then-new type of dinosaur. The specimen was collected near Denver and described by Othniel C. Marsh in 1890 who named it

Ornithomimus and recognized it as a new type of theropod. It was not until 1917 that enough of the skeleton of these dinosaurs was discovered to show that they were toothless, fleet footed beasts who may have eaten anything they could run down or scavenge. Ornithomimosaurs were similar in size to ostriches and like them their bones were hollow. A very apparent major difference is that bird-mimic dinosaurs have long slender arms with hands well developed for grasping. Perhaps because of their omnivorous diet they used their slender arms to pull down fruited branches

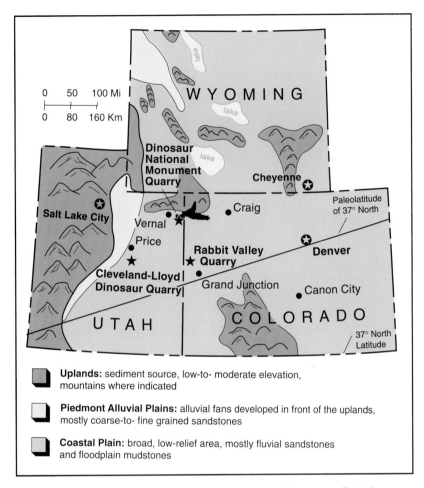

0   50   100 Mi

0   80   160 Km

W Y O M I N G

lake

lake

lake

Dinosaur
National
Monument
Quarry

Cheyenne

Salt Lake City

Vernal

Craig

Price

Paleolatitude
of 37° North

Rabbit Valley
Quarry

Denver

Cleveland-Lloyd
Dinosaur Quarry

Grand Junction

Canon City

U T A H

C O L O R A D O

37° North
Latitude

Uplands: sediment source, low-to- moderate elevation, mountains where indicated

Piedmont Alluvial Plains: alluvial fans developed in front of the uplands, mostly coarse-to- fine grained sandstones

Coastal Plain: broad, low-relief area, mostly fluvial sandstones and floodplain mudstones

Figure 60. By 70-million years ago near the end of the Cretaceous Period mountain building forces were at work throughout Utah, Colorado, and Wyoming and the entire state was once again above sea level.

from plants or to catch lizards and insects. Another major difference between birds and ornithomimosaurs was that these dinosaurs had a long tail which they carried erect. The tail acted as a counterbalance when the ornithomimid was running. The hind legs of these speedy dinosaurs were long and powerful like those of the ostrich, but terminated in a three toed foot much like that of the other theropod dinosaurs.

Fossils from other dinosaurs featured in Figure 61 have been found

in other Late Cretaceous rocks outside of Colorado. One of these, the bony plated quadruped in the left foreground of Figure 61, is one of the ankylosaurids or armored dinosaurs. This herbivore relied on its heavy bony plating as protection from the carnivores of the time. With their heavy, squat, low slung bodies, these dinosaurs certainly could not outrun any of the swift predators of the Late Cretaceous. For defense they may have hunkered down much as a porcupine does today when faced with an attack from a carnivore.

Other dinosaurs pictured in Figure 61 include hadrosaurs featured in the upper left middle ground and a tyrannosaurid (the family of carnivorous dinosaurs including *Tyrannosaurus rex* and *Albertosaurus*) silhouetted in the center background. Although no fossils of *Albertosaurus* have yet been found in Late Cretaceous deposits in Colorado, we know that these dinosaurs formed part of the fauna present during the Late Cretaceous. Both hadrosaurs and tyrannosaurids, including *Tyrannosaurus rex,* have been found in the Black Hills of South Dakota and the northeastern corner of Wyoming. *Tyrannosaurus rex* was recently discovered in Colorado, south of Dinosaur Ridge.

As the Cretaceous came to a close, so did the reign of the dinosaurs. The Tertiary, the time period which immediately follows the Cretaceous, is often referred to as the Age of Mammals. Today a popular theory for the extinction of the dinosaurs and many other animal groups is that an extraterrestrial event, such as a collision with a large meteor, asteroid, or comet, occurred at or near the Cretaceous-Tertiary boundary.

If such a large scale catastrophic event did occur, it seems likely that evidence for this collision should be easy to find in the rocks. Such is not the case. There are only a few places in the world where there is a continuous rock record of the transition between the Cretaceous and Tertiary time periods. Most of this record is found in rocks that were deposited in

Figure 61. Life as it may have appeared around what is now Denver only 5-million years before the dinosaurs became extinct.

the marine environment, and it is difficult to extrapolate any data found here to the terrestrial environment.

As scientists began to study the rocks that straddle the boundary between the Cretaceous and Tertiary they found that rocks from some of the study areas had an increased amount of iridium, a heavy metallic element which is related to platinum and is often associated with meteorites. This anomalously high concentration of iridium occurred in rocks at the boundary between the Cretaceous and Tertiary. In addition, a variety of quartz, called shocked quartz, which is indicative of an explosive event, has been found.

Iridium and shocked quartz are *indirect* evidence of a possible collision of the earth with a large meteor, asteroid or comet, but they are *direct* evidence of an explosive event.

Scientists have not been satisfied with this indirect evidence of a possible extraterrestrial event. Still controversial evidence of an impact crater has been found in the Caribbean where geophysicists have found indications of a deeply buried circular crater 115-miles (192 kilometers) wide. This possible impact site is located in the Caribbean off the west coast of the Yucatán peninsula. It is buried beneath the present day surface and appears to be of the

right age to be the main suspect. Although not common, other buried impact craters from meteor collisions occur throughout the world.

Other geologists who are searching for more direct evidence of a catastrophic collision are studying non-marine rocks deposited across the Cretaceous and Tertiary boundary. Researchers are now examining plant and animal fossils which were living as the Cretaceous came to an end and the Tertiary was commencing. Plant microfossils, in the form of pollen and spores, appear to be quite promising sources of data for resolving this controversy. In the western interior of the United States, these tiny fossils indicate that a catastrophic event may have taken place at or near the boundary between the Cretaceous and Tertiary. Immediately above the Cretaceous-Tertiary boundary there is a thin zone where fern spores are very abundant. This thin layer suggests ferns may have been initially recolonizing a devastated landscape. This has been seen at Krakatoa, a now dormant volcanic island located in Indonesia. When Krakatoa erupted in 1883 it literally destroyed the island. After the eruption, ferns were the first plants to recolonize the landscape. Although this evidence is again indirect, it does help to confirm that an explosive event of worldwide proportion may have affected the earth's plant and animal communities at the end of the Cretaceous.

It may sound like geologists are now on the verge of discovering the proverbial smoking gun in the dinosaur extinction case. Although the case may be nearing a solution, many problems still remain. Much of the analytical chemical data used is measured in parts per trillion and may not be scientifically significant. There is also the problem of how reliable is it to make worldwide assumptions about climatic and/or catastrophic events based upon only a few study areas located thousands of miles or kilometers apart.

Although at least one suspect site for an impact crater of the right age has been found, there has still not been any direct evidence that such a crater exists. The process of erosion over the past 65-million

years could have easily obscured a crater, whether that crater be on land or in the oceans of the world.

Whether geologists favor a gradual or catastrophic extinction of the dinosaurs, they are all concentrating their research on the Cretaceous-Tertiary boundary. Two areas within Colorado (Figure 62) are the focus of some of the research. At these sites there is a continuous rock record across the Cretaceous and Tertiary boundary. They are areas which were downwarped while mountains were uplifted to the west. One site is west of Denver on the edge of the Denver Basin. Here the Denver Formation, discussed in earlier chapters, straddles the boundary between the Cretaceous and Tertiary. Besides containing dinosaur fossils in the lower portion and Tertiary mammals and plants in the upper part, rocks of the Denver Formation show that this area of Colorado was undergoing an episode of volcanism during the latest Cretaceous and on into the Tertiary. The volcanic ash and lava flows (Figure 63) could have had an adverse effect on a local

dinosaur population. If this volcanism was as active worldwide as it was around the Denver area, it may have contributed to the extinction of the dinosaurs. Rocks of the Denver Formation do not contain any iridium, shocked quartz or anomalous associations of pollen and spores which might help scientists argue more conclusively for an extraterrestrial collision at the end of the Cretaceous.

Further to the south, rocks in the Raton Basin of south central Colorado (Figure 62) contain a variety of evidence which may be used to support either the theory of extraterrestrial collision or increased volcanism as a cause of the extinctions. In the Raton Basin scientists have found higher than normal concentrations of iridium at the Cretaceous-Tertiary boundary and samples of shocked quartz, both indirect evidence of a possible collision and direct evidence of an explosive event. In addition, microscopic fossilized plant pollen and spores indicate that an abrupt change occurred in plant communities at the boundary, with a dramatic

Figure 62. Location of the Denver and Raton Basins in Colorado where rocks were deposited continuously across the boundary between the Cretaceous and Tertiary Periods.

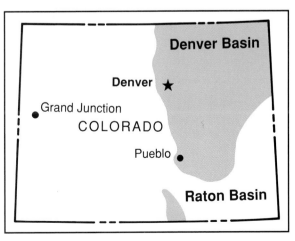

increase in ferns immediately above the Cretaceous rocks. A change in the composition of the plant communities could result from a number of causes, including an extraterrestrial collision, a large scale episode of volcanism or a shift in climatic patterns. It should be noted that rocks of the Raton Basin do contain evidence of active volcanism, much like the rocks in the Denver Basin.

Many other theories on dinosaur extinctions have been postulated, including worldwide disease epidemics, a drastic change in the makeup of the plant communities or a change in the worldwide climate which dinosaurs and other animals and plants could not adapt to. The real cause of the extinction of the dinosaurs and other animals and plants for the present remains a mystery.

It needs to be emphasized that although the extinctions at the Cretaceous-Tertiary boundary are currently a popular topic, other

Figure 63. A view looking east from Lookout Mountain toward the Denver Basin (east of Golden, Colorado) where sedimentary rocks of the Denver Formation are interbedded with lava flows (cliff forming unit).

episodes of mass extinctions occurred several times in the earth's history. Throughout the 600-million-year history of life on earth there have been numerous times when extinctions have decimated plant and animal communities. Extinction is certainly a common fate which has affected the vast majority of the earth's plants and animals. These other extinctions have not received as much attention because the plants and animals involved have not been as spectacular as dinosaurs.

THE SEARCH GOES ON

TODAY both the mystique of past fabulous discoveries and the promise of new and hopefully unique dinosaur fossils attracts paleontologists from Colorado, other states and even the world to the extensive Mesozoic rocks of Colorado. People from many different academic institutions are always anxious to see what new discovery may await their slow and meticulous process of excavation. In many cases, avid amateur paleontologists offer their assistance and enthusiasm to these projects.

Today's paleontologists use the same method of excavating dinosaur bones for transportation which was developed in the 1800s. They still slowly expose the often fragile bones and then apply a wrap that will protect the fossils during their transport back to the home base of the paleontologists. However the technique of exposing the bones has undergone a great technological jump. Heavy equipment such as bulldozers or tools such as jack hammers are sometimes used to remove the rock layers which overly the bones. Once the excavation nears the bones, smaller tools, such as whisk brooms, paint brushes, and even dental tools (Figure 64) are used to clean the sediment from the bones. Next the bones are commonly soaked with a hardener before they

are jacketed with plaster bandages. Prior to applying several layers of the plaster bandages, a veneer of tissue paper is applied over the bones so the plaster soaked bandages will not adhere to the fossils. Next several layers of plaster soaked burlap bandages are applied to protect the fossils during transportation. Today the long trip of the bandaged bones back to the museum is again helped by present day technology. Instead of wagon trains or ferry boats (see Chapter 2, Figure 9) helicopters are sometimes used to transport the heavy jackets out of localities with limited access (Figure 65).

Much of today's study of dinosaurs focuses on Colorado's Western Slope near the town of Grand Junction and at Dinosaur National Monument (Figure 66) where paleontologists are making some new and unique discoveries. One site, the Fruita Paleontological Area, is immediately west of Grand Junction on land owned by the U.S. Government. Both the Museum of Western Colorado, located in downtown Grand Junction, and California State University in Long Beach have been working closely with the U.S. Bureau of Land Management (BLM) to collect and study

Figure 64. The partial skeleton of a stegosaur has been exposed and awaits the application of a plaster jacket before it is transported to a museum. Note the stegosaur tail spikes to the right of the rectangular pan in the upper center of the photograph.

Figure 65. Sometimes the terrain is so rough at present day dinosaur quarries that helicopters are used to transport the heavy plaster jacketed bones from the field to the museum. Here a helicopter from the Colorado National Guard awaits in the background while researchers from the Museum of Western Colorado prepare the plaster jacketed bones for transport.

dinosaur and other fossils found in the Jurassic Morrison Formation.

The Fruita Paleontological Area encompasses a fairly large badlands (Figure 67) where dinosaur bones, mostly disarticulated, occur in the base of sandstones which were deposited by ancient streams. This site is unusual because in the finer grained rocks of the ancient floodplain, many microfossils have been discovered. These tiny fossils have to be identified with the aid of a binocular microscope. They are the much smaller lizards, amphibians, fish and plants (Figure 68) which lived alongside dinosaurs around 140-million years ago. In some cases these tiny fossils may be the nearly complete skeletons of smaller vertebrates. This is the area where the tiny dinosaur *Echinodon* was discovered (see Chapter 6). Microvertebrate fossils from this site are being studied by ama-

teur and professional paleontologists from California State while paleontologists from Dinosaur Valley, part of the Museum of Western Colorado, have been involved with the collection and curation of the larger vertebrates. Their most unique discovery has been the skull of *Ceratosaurus*, one of the large carnivores which possessed nasal horns (see Chapter 6, Figure 49).

Almost at the Utah border, more dinosaur bones were discovered by amateur paleontologists in 1981 who reported their find to the Museum of Western Colorado. This site, again on federal land, is just north of the exit for Rabbit Valley from Interstate 70 and is referred to as the Mygatt-Moore Dinosaur Quarry (Figure 69), in honor of the people who discovered the site. The bones occur in a bentonite-rich mudstone which is overlain by fine-

Figure 66. Sites on Colorado's Western Slope of major recent research projects for studying fossils.

Figure 67. A view of the badlands of the Fruita Paleontological Area west of Grand Junction and southwest of Fruita. In the center of the photograph, students from the Colorado School of Mines are working on excavating a dinosaur bone.

grained shales deposited in an ancient lake. A few small fish skeletons have turned up in the lake deposits. Researchers from Dinosaur Valley and interested amateurs, both local and from around the United States, continue to excavate mostly large dinosaur bones. Most common are bones from large Jurassic sauropods including *Apatosaurus* (*Brontosaurus*), *Camarasaurus* and possibly *Brachiosaurus*. Bones and teeth belonging to *Allosaurus,* a common large predator of the Jurassic, have also been found. Some bones might belong to *Stegosaurus,* Colorado's State Fossil.

An intriguing discovery during the summer field season of 1990 was some dermal scutes (bony plates in the skin) from an ankylosaurid (the armored dinosaurs). Although these fossils still await a formal descrip-

Figure 69. Researchers from the Museum of Western Colorado and students from the Colorado School of Mines in Golden, Colorado toil away at the Mygatt-Moore Dinosaur Quarry.

tion, they have already been discussed in several newspaper articles. This is the first occurrence of these armored dinosaurs in the Jurassic Morrison Formation in Colorado. Other vertebrates found at this site include fish and a turtle. As is often the case with dinosaur bonebeds, bones and teeth at the Mygatt-Moore Dinosaur Quarry are disarticulated and scattered throughout the fossiliferous rock layer. Researchers are faced with a complex three dimensional jigsaw puzzle as they attempt to reconstruct skeletons after the bones are transported back to the museum.

Scientists from Dinosaur Valley, the paleontology section of the Museum of Western Colorado, are taking many of the specimens they have collected and are using them in an applied research project both in the field and back at the museum.

They have been working side by side with paleontologists from Dinamation International, a company which manufactures lifelike robot dinosaurs. All of these people have been busily studying how specimens from the Mygatt-Moore quarry fit in the context of new ideas of dinosaur behavior, then constructing exhibits in the museum that inform the public not only of the rich cache of dinosaur fossils in the Grand Junction area, but also what their specimens show about the lives of the dinosaurs. In the field, museum personnel, along with the help of many interested volunteers and the BLM, have been preparing interpretive trails that help people relive some of the early discoveries made during 1900 and 1901. These interpretive trails also educate the public about how unique and nonrenewable dinosaur fossils are.

Figure 68. Plant debris found in fine-grained sediments of the Morrison Formation at the Fruita Paleontological Area. The rock here has been broken in two to show the plant fossils.

Between Grand Junction and the town of Delta, Colorado (Figure 66) a unique discovery has occurred in the lower portion of the Morrison Formation. This is the site where Dr. Robert Young and two Egyptian geologists discovered the fossilized reptile nest and fossil eggs shown in Figure 46 of Chapter 6. Dr. Young has used his observations of the layering of the nest, the variety of animal and plant microfossils and the thousands of egg fragments to come up with the interpretation that this was the nest of a dinosaur, perhaps *Ornitholestes,* which occupied the nest site several times and brought prey back to its young. *Ornitholestes* was an active bipedal coelurosaur whose bones have been found at other Jurassic sites in the western United States, the closest site being the Dry Mesa Dinosaur Quarry which lies about 17 miles (27.5 kilometers) south-southwest of the Young Egg Site.

Both the Young Egg Site and the Dry Mesa Dinosaur Quarry are south of Grand Junction near the town of Delta, Colorado (Figure 66). At Dry Mesa, paleontologists from Brigham Young University in Provo, Utah have been excavating Jurassic dinosaur fossils from the Morrison Formation. They have been working this quarry off and on since the 1970s and tons of bones have been retrieved from the site. Dr. Wade Miller and Ken Stadtman, both from BYU, are currently in charge of the project where they have received assistance from many of the geology students at BYU. Some of Dry Mesa's fossils are currently on display at the BYU Earth Science Museum in Provo,

Utah. Like the Mygatt-Moore Dinosaur Quarry, fossilized bones of *Apatosaurus* (*Brontosaurus*), *Diplodocus, Brachiosaurus* and *Camarasaurus* (all sauropods) are common. The Dry Mesa Dinosaur Quarry is unique for it has yielded bones of the world's second and third largest dinosaurs. These two dinosaurs, both sauropods probably related to *Brachiosaurus,* are *Ultrasaurus* (second place) and *Supersaurus* (third place). These dinosaurs are discussed in more detail in Chapter 4.

During years of excavation at the Dry Mesa Quarry many different types of dinosaurs were discovered. Most well represented are the saurischian, or lizard-hipped dinosaurs. Besides a large contingent of sauropods mentioned in the preceding paragraph, Dry Mesa has yielded numerous fossils of the two types of theropod or beast-foot dinosaurs. Carnosaurs (see Chapter 4), or flesh eaters, from three families are represented. *Allosaurus,* a member of the allosaurid family, a common predator of the Jurassic, has been found. Two other families, the megalosaurids, as exemplified by *Ceratosaurus* and *Torvosaurus* and a probable tyrannosaurid, *Stokesosaurus* have been identified.

Coelurosaurids, a second type of theropod, or beast-foot dinosaur, characterized by their hollow bird-like bones, are not quite as common as the other theropods. So far partial skeletons of two bird-mimic dinosaurs, *Ornitholestes* and *Coelurus* have been identified. Another coelurosaurid found is called *Marshosaurus*. This dinosaur is one of the dromeosaurs, or running lizards,

which are characterized by an over-size claw on their hind feet, a slender body built for running, and a large head with powerful jaws.

Ornithischian, or bird-hipped, dinosaurs did not enjoy their heyday until the Cretaceous and indeed fossils found at Dry Mesa Quarry help substantiate this fact. To date only three and possibly four different types of ornithischians have turned up in the ongoing excavation. Three of these reptiles are ornithopods, or bird-foot, dinosaurs. This large group includes some of the early types of fleet-footed ornithopods which had different shaped teeth in their jaws. A dinosaur called *Dryosaurus* and perhaps one called *Othnelia* have been found at Dry Mesa. The third ornithopod is a common Jurassic herbivore called *Camptosaurus. Camptosaurus* is a member of a family of ornithopods called iguanodontids. Iguanodontids are characterized by having teeth like a present day iguana and thumbs on the forelimbs modified into spikes which were probably used for defense.

A final constituent of the Dry Mesa ornithischian clan is *Stegosaurus,* a dinosaur that everyone usually recognizes because of its tiny head, a humped or rounded back with rows of bony plates, and bony spikes projecting from the end of its tail. The Jurassic was the heyday of the stegosaurids, who for as yet an unknown reason, vanished from the scene during the Cretaceous, long before the massive extinction at the Cretaceous-Tertiary boundary killed off the dinosaurs and many other animals and plants. Although parts and pieces of stegosaurs have been found several times in Colorado's Morrison Formation, only a few nearly complete skeletons have been discovered, thus leading to many unanswered questions about this group (see Chapter 4).

From the Grand Junction area it is only a short journey of around 125 miles (208 kilometers) to another Western Slope site in the northwestern corner of Colorado. This world famous site is Dinosaur National Monument. This site is unique because its scenic splendor and dinosaur quarry are open to the public. Every year around 250,000 people visit this National Monument managed by the National Park Service. Instead of removing the dinosaur bones, researchers at Dinosaur National Monument are busy exposing bones in the quarry for the public to see them in situ in the rocks which have entombed them for so many millions of years.

Dinosaur National Monument's quarry is located on the western side of the monument, north of the town of Jensen, Utah, only 12.5 miles (20 kilometers) due west of the Colorado border (Figure 66). This site is another rich treasure chest of Jurassic Morrison Formation dinosaur bones. Like other sites on Colorado's Western Slope, the dinosaur fauna is dominated by large sauropods, including *Diplodocus*, *Apatosaurus* (*Brontosaurus*), and *Camarasaurus*. Another large sauropod called *Barosaurus* has also been found. Two types of carnivorous saurischian dinosaurs, *Allosaurus* and *Ceratosaurus*, occur in the quarry.

Figure 70. Along Colorado's Front Range, the once horizontal beds of the Jurassic Morrison Formation (variegated gray and red beds in the right two-thirds of the photograph) have been tilted steeply in response to mountain building.

As is the case at other Jurassic dinosaur quarries throughout Colorado, ornithischian or bird-hipped dinosaurs are relatively rare at Dinosaur National Monument. To date the bones of three kinds, *Stegosaurus*, *Dryosaurus* and *Camptosaurus* have been excavated and identified.

Within the monument boundaries, but away from the public eye, scientists are busy with exploratory expeditions and collecting a variety of primitive mammals and other fossils. Perhaps these sites or their fossils will be incorporated into the exhibits at the monument in the future.

East of Dinosaur National Monument in the vicinity of Craig, Colorado researchers led by Dr. David Archibald from San Diego State University in San Diego, California are busy collecting and studying fossils of small mammals which lived literally underfoot of dinosaurs during the Cretaceous, the period of geologic time immediately after the Jurassic. Professors and students are busy sifting through the ancient sediments that were deposited around 80-million years ago as the once vast epicontinental seaway began to retreat from Colorado. In their search for fossil mammals they have discovered a few bones of a yet unidentified hadrosaur (duckbill). Perhaps their further exploration will be rewarded with the discovery of a Cretaceous dinosaur bone bed that would be as rich as bone beds found in the Morrison Formation.

Dinosaur researchers are busy along the eastern flank of the central ridge of mountains which separates Colorado's Western Slope from its eastern prairies as well as further east onto the prairies. Here along the Front Range the once horizontal layers of sediments are tilted more than 45 degrees (Figure 70) due to a mountain building episode which started in the Cretaceous near the end of the reign of the dinosaurs. Researchers have an advantage with this geologic setting for a thicker portion of the strata is exposed in a smaller area. Search parties can therefore explore more of the exposed rocks in a shorter length of time. However, problems sometimes arise because the dinosaur skeleton will also be tilted and may be more difficult to remove for it quickly dips below the surface. When Othniel Marsh collected north of the town of Morrison in the late 1800s his crew had to prop up the overlying rocks in order to dig into the hillside and recover the fossils.

Today in eastern Colorado dinosaur research revolves around Marsh and Cope's initial sites which started the rush to America's dinosaurs. North of Canon City in Garden Park people from the BLM, the Garden Park Paleontological Society, and the Denver Museum of Natural History are involved in a multi-faceted research project. Here people from the BLM (Bureau of Land Management), amateur and professional paleontologists have banded together to assess the remaining paleontological merit of the area, identify the historical quarry sites, collect fossils for research and erect informative plaques about the area's geology and paleontology. To date most of Cope's old quarries, Marsh's productive quarry and the quarry opened by the Cleveland Museum

of Natural History have been located (see Chapter 2, Figure 4), signs which commemorate the paleontological importance are being prepared and when time permits, volunteers are exploring the area for more dinosaur fossils.

The Garden Park Paleontological Society has announced plans to build a tourist information center at Garden Park. It is unique in Colorado for its continuous record of dinosaur life and the number of complete or nearly complete *Stegosaurus* fossils. The July 1993 discovery of several dinosaur eggs marks it as one of only six or seven Jurassic nest sites in the United States.

To the north near Denver, activity by both amateurs and professionals is currently focused on a portion of the Dakota Hogback bounded by Interstate 70 on the north and on the south by the town of Morrison (Figure 71). Within this 3-mile (4.8 kilometer) exposure of steeply dip-

ping beds of the Morrison Formation and the Dakota Group lie the dinosaur quarries which Marsh and his men worked in the late 1870s and dinosaur trackways first documented in the 1930s by researchers from the Denver Museum of Natural History. Bones and dinosaur trackways are still visible in places along the ridge. Besides having significance for anyone interested in paleontology, Dinosaur Ridge has ecological significance for it is in the transition zone between the mountain and plain ecosystems. This site is also a locale for prehistoric archaeological discoveries.

Dr. Martin Lockley, a professor of geology at the University of Colorado at Denver has been instrumental in focusing public attention on this ridge. He and his students initially mapped the trackways exposed along the ridge and called for the need to preserve the historical and present day resources of this

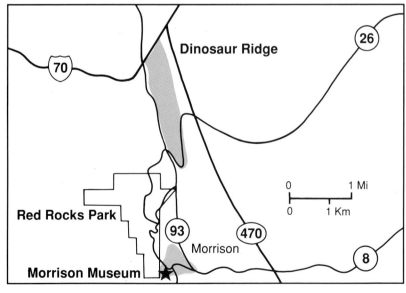

Figure 71. Location map of Dinosaur Ridge.

Figure 72. A cross section of a rib (upper portion of photo) and a portion of a limb bone of a dinosaur at Dinosaur Ridge.

ence of more ceratopsian (horned) dinosaurs in the Late Cretaceous rocks of the Denver and Laramie Formations and have discovered a Jurassic predatory theropod larger than *Allosaurus,* the most common predator of the Jurassic. This dinosaur, called *Epanterias,* was discovered north of Denver near the city of Fort Collins in the Morrison Formation. Little is known about *Epanterias,* because previously only fragmentary remains have been discovered.

A unique site of current research lies in the southeastern corner of Colorado (see Chapter 6, Figure 51) where dinosaur trackways in the Morrison Formation were first reported in 1938, along with some preliminary collecting. The Morrison Formation is best known for its dinosaur bones, but this large exposure of tracks has served as an excellent site for investigating Jurassic dinosaur behavior. Studies by

locale. A group called the Friends of Dinosaur Ridge has now formed and is actively working toward the goal of setting the area aside as a park where the dinosaur trackways will be preserved, and the area's historical paleontological significance can be brought to the public's attention. Fortunately a vast majority of the acreage within this proposed park is already in the public domain. Today's major problem is addressing the closing of a road which travels uphill through the beds of the Morrison Formation on the west side. This road makes a hairpin turn at the crest of the ridge and goes downhill through the rocks of the Dakota Group on the eastern side. Dinosaur bones are still visible in the rocks of the Morrison Formation (Figure 72) and dinosaur footprints can be seen in the Dakota Group (Figure 73). This and other areas are discussed in detail in Chapter 9.

Up the road from Denver, researchers from the University of Colorado at Boulder, are carrying on investigations along the Front Range. In the last few years Dr. Robert Bakker and his associates have cited the pres-

Figure 73. A trackway of the hind feet of an ornithischian iguanodontid dinosaur made over 100-million years ago when this area was a flat lying beach. The footprints were brushed with water to improve the contrast between the print and the surrounding rock.

Dr. Martin Lockley from the University of Colorado at Denver and his students have helped to document a current interpretation that some dinosaurs traveled in herds. In this case the dinosaurs were traveling parallel to an ancient shoreline of a large lake. Different size sauropod tracks were probably made by adult and juvenile dinosaurs. Solitary predatory dinosaurs may have been following the herd looking for easy prey among the young or sick dinosaurs.

Both the Denver Museum of Natural History and the University of Colorado Museum in the Henderson Building on the Boulder Campus have ongoing research projects related to Colorado's dinosaurs. Both of these institutions are involved in presenting some of their research to their patrons by updating and adding new exhibits. They are using specimens, or casts of them, they have collected on their expeditions and are incorporating them into new displays. Through models and skeletal mounts these exhibits show dinosaurs actively interacting with their environment and other dinosaurs. They reflect new ideas on the dynamic social behavior of the dinosaurs.

At the Denver Museum of Natural History people interested in what happens to fossils after collection and before the final exhibit can have a firsthand view of the process at the museum's new paleontological preparation laboratory. This state of the art laboratory was completed early in 1990. It features viewing windows where visitors can see how museum specialists prepare, reconstruct specimens and often make casts of the specimens for display (Figure 74).

Although each paleontologist from the many institutions conducting research on Colorado's dinosaurs has his or her own special project, all are interested in preserving these relics of the past for future generations. In some cases these fossils can not be collected in their entirety, as is the case with the dinosaur trackways in southeastern Colorado. However, researchers can document the presence of these vast discoveries through mapping and photography, thus preserving them for future study and appreciation. If any readers are interested in helping with dinosaur research or feel they have unearthed a fossil from the Mesozoic, they should contact a local academic institution.

Amateur collectors must keep in mind that certain laws apply to the collection of dinosaur or other fossils. Depending on where the fossil is found it may fall on private, state or federal property. Local institutions usually have the appropriate permits in hand so they can lawfully collect on any of these lands. This is one reason why many amateur dinosaur researchers work with an institution. Another reason is that few amateurs would have available to them the tremendous amount of workers and equipment needed to excavate a dinosaur skeleton.

Whatever an amateur's motivation may be, professional paleontologists are usually happy to receive their help. It often means that professional researchers may be able to accomplish more than their initial meager budget or finite amount of time would allow.

Figure 74. View of the paleontological laboratory at the Denver Museum of Natural History. Here Phyllis Kincade prepares to make a mold of the vertebra of an extinct plesiosaur, a seagoing reptile which lived at the same time as dinosaurs.

TOUR GUIDE TO COLORADO'S DINOSAURS

P RESENT DAY EXPLORERS can start investigating dinosaurs almost anywhere in Colorado. Colorado is fortunate in having several attractions that are open to the public. They range from the obvious, museums which celebrate Colorado's rich dinosaur heritage and many discoveries made in the state to the more obscure attractions which include interpretive trails and college courses open to the public. These many attractions are concentrated in two areas of the state, the Front Range, centered around Denver (Figure 75) and Colorado's Western Slope, centered around Grand Junction (Figure 76). Addresses and telephone numbers are provided at the end of the chapter for those who want more information.

If in your explorations you feel you have discovered a dinosaur fossil, your find should be reported to the nearest institution. This will assure that your possibly rare discovery is properly excavated and all pertinent ancillary information is collected along with the specimen. Many of today's dinosaur researchers are more than happy to work with an interested amateur, and the experience is often rewarding to both the scientist and the amateur.

Along the Front Range, explorers can retrace the footprints of Oth-

niel C. Marsh and Edward D. Cope through visiting sites west of Denver and north of Canon City. Marsh's main area of quarrying is now referred to as Dinosaur Ridge and is located north of the town of Morrison, Colorado (Figure 75). This is the famous historical site initially discovered by Arthur Lakes and excavated by Othniel C. Marsh in 1877 (see Chapter 2). Amateur and professional geologists and paleontologists have produced a guidebook about Dinosaur Ridge which points out the area's many geological and paleontological resources (see page 72 for details). Dinosaur Ridge can be reached by proceeding west from Denver on Interstate 70 to the exit for Golden, Colorado and State Highway 26/Jefferson County Road 93. Take this exit, which is immediately after a large roadcut and turn south on Highway 26/Road 93. After passing under the I-70 overpass visitors can take a

left hand turn 0.1 mile (0.06 Kilometer) south to view the point of geologic interest which is a roadcut through the Hogback that was made for I-70. There is signage along the outcrop which points out the various strata and talks about what events took place millions of years ago. From here visitors should return to Highway 26/Road 93 and proceed south for 1.4 (2.3 kilometers) miles to the junction where State Highway 26 (Alameda Parkway) turns to the east. Make a left turn onto the

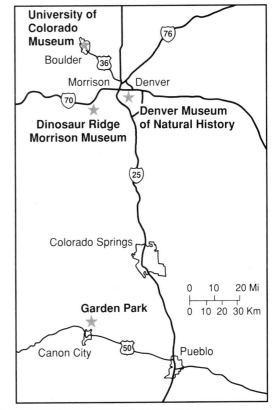

Figure 75. Sites related to dinosaurs are open to the public along Colorado's Front Range.

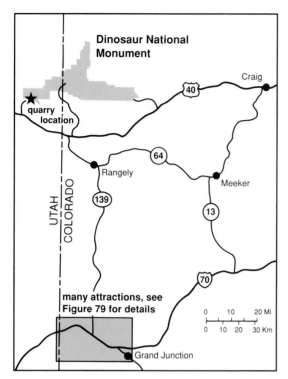

many attractions, see
Figure 79 for details

Figure 76. Many educational attractions related to dinosaurs can also be found on Colorado's Western Slope.

highway and proceed up the backside or scree slope of Dinosaur Ridge. Near the top of the ridge the road makes a sharp hairpin turn and the traveler then finds himself traveling downhill along the dip slope of the Cretaceous Dakota Group (Figure 77).

As you travel up and then down Dinosaur Ridge, you will first see the multi-colored and often discontinuous sandstones and shales of the world famous Morrison Formation. Although Marsh and his crew removed most of the dinosaur bones, a keen-eyed visitor will notice that a few bones are still in the rock (see Figure 72, Chapter 8). These bones are the few remaining isolated fossils that were not worth collecting from the well-cemented Morrison sandstones. Please note that it is unlawful to collect any fossils in this area. Today this area is protected and patrolled so that others may share the thrill of discovering a dinosaur fossil in the Morrison Formation. The numbered posts you encounter along the route are to be used in conjunction with the guidebook to the area. This guidebook not only discusses dinosaur fossils, but also the general geology of Dinosaur Ridge. Some of the highlights include: a) dinosaur bones in the outcrop of the Morrison Formation and in boulders along the west side of the road on the west side of Dinosaur Ridge, b) the unconformity between the Jurassic and Cretaceous rocks and many trace fossils such as worm burrows, c) and dinosaur tracks in the Cretaceous rocks of the Dakota Group.

While in the vicinity of Denver a stop at the Denver Museum of Natural History is a must. This museum is east of downtown Denver and features full size skeletal mounts of dinosaurs, Cretaceous marine reptiles, Cenozoic mammals and educational exhibits about the history of life on earth. A paleontological preparation laboratory is a great educational display. In this room of the museum, visitors can view museum paleontologists and technicians working on the preparation and reconstruction of fossils (Figure 78).

Figure 77. An aerial view of Dinosaur Ridge looking north shows Alameda Parkway as it climbs the ridge through the rocks of the Jurassic Morrison Formation (left) and then descends past the rocks of the Cretaceous Dakota Group (right).

Figure 78. The new paleontological laboratory at the Denver Museum of Natural History.

In a different area of the museum, two dinosaurs from famous research sites are on display. One, a *Stegosaurus,* is from Garden Park and the other, *Diplodocus,* comes from Dinosaur National Monument. A third dinosaur, *Allosaurus,* from the area near Dinosaur National Monument was being prepared for exhibit at the writing of this book. Other dinosaurs on display at this writing are *Tyrannosaurus rex* and *Edmontosaurus,* a duckbilled ornithopod. The Denver Museum of Natural History has the distinction of being the only museum in the United States west of the Mississippi River that has mounted skeletons of four well known dinosaurs. The museum is open daily and an admission is charged.

From Denver it is only a short drive north to the campus of the University of Colorado at Boulder where more displays await the explorer in search of Colorado's dinosaur story (Figure 75). Dr. Robert Bakker, one of the researchers on the campus and most noted for his book, *The Dinosaur Heresies,* has helped develop a series of exhibits along the theme of dinosaurs and sea monsters of the ancient Rocky Mountains. Visitors to the geology wing of the University of Colorado Museum in the Henderson Building are treated to a well integrated and dynamic series of exhibits including murals depicting galloping dinosaurs and active marine reptiles. Informative exhibits discuss dinosaur social behavior. Admission to the museum located on the west side of the campus near 15th Street and Broadway is free as is parking on the weekends.

Adventurers can next head south from the Denver metro area on Interstate 25 to obtain a first hand look at Colorado's second, and equally important site, which attracted Othniel Marsh and Edward Cope to the state in 1877 (Figure 75). Garden Park is on the way to the Royal Gorge, one of Colorado's many scenic attractions where the Arkansas River has cut a deep and beautiful canyon into the Precambrian rocks of the Front Range. At the Royal Gorge a suspension bridge over the gorge offers breathtaking views of the canyon. To reach this area visitors should head west on U.S. Highway 50 from Pueblo, Colorado to the town of Canon City. Garden Park Fossil Area is about 8 miles (12.9 kilometers) north of town on County Highway 9 (be careful here for there is a Colorado State Highway 9 also in the area).

People may want to check with the Chamber of Commerce in Canon City to obtain more detailed information about current dinosaur attractions in the area. In the past, the BLM (U.S. Bureau of Land Management), the Garden Park Paleontological Society and other interested people have led tours in Garden Park during the summer months. Even if tours are not available at the time of a visit, the scenic views of the colorful Jurassic Morrison Formation and other rocks is worth the drive. A couple of old monuments are in place along the road that commemorate Garden Park's dinosaur discoveries. At the writing of this book more signage was planned. Dinosaur resources of

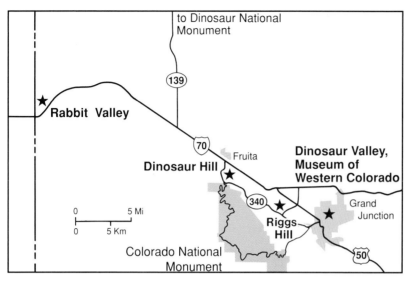

Figure 79. Sites near Grand Junction, Colorado, where several dinosaur attractions are open to the public.

the area are currently under development and changes are taking place with every tourist season.

In southeast Colorado is the Picket Wire Canyonlands which became part of the Comanche National Grasslands in 1991. In this canyon along the Purgatoire River is the longest set of dinosaur tracks found in the world (see Figure 51). There are also archeological sites in the area. At Pueblo, turn southeast on U.S. Highway 50 to La Junta, then head southeast again on Highway 109. Access to this area is complicated and a high clearance vehicle is needed. The Forest Service offers guided tours and information on how to get there.

Many attractions related to dinosaurs can be found around Grand Junction (Figure 79). This area holds much for both the outdoor enthusiast and aficionados of museums and interpretive displays. In the early 1980s a cooperative project

between the Museum of Western Colorado in Grand Junction and the Bureau of Land Management (BLM) began to take shape. The fruits of this cooperative venture were the construction of three self-guided interpretive trails which visit two of Elmer Riggs' 1900 dinosaur quarries and one present day research site. All of these trails are laid out over the scenic badlands topography of the Jurassic Morrison Formation.

Near Grand Junction visitors may examine one of the many quarries opened by Elmer Riggs at a locality called Riggs Hill (Figure 79). This site lies immediately west of Grand Junction and may be reached from Interstate 70 by taking the exit for Number 24 Road (the exit after Horizon Drive if you are heading west, or the first exit for Grand Junction if you are heading east). Proceed south on Number 24 Road until you reach the intersection with Redlands Parkway. Head west

(a right turn) on Redlands Parkway and it will change names to South Broadway after you pass the intersection of Redlands Parkway and Broadway. Continue south and South Broadway will curve toward the west. You will then first pass the intersection with South Camp Road and then Meadows Way. Parking for Riggs Hill is immediately past the Meadows Way intersection on the north side of South Broadway. There is a sign easily visible from here which marks the trailhead.

At the trailhead explorers will want to check the mailbox on the trailhead sign to see if any trail guides are available. These guides offer explanations to the eight numbered stops along the trail and point out the significance of the quarry where Riggs discovered the first partial skeleton of what at the time was the world's largest dinosaur, *Brachiosaurus altithorax,* a sauropod. If the box which usually contains the trail guide is empty, copies of the guide may be purchased at Dinosaur Valley, the Museum of Western Colorado's dinosaur museum located in Grand Junction. The eight numbered stops take visitors to Riggs' old quarry, marked by a commemorative plaque, and then to another quarry that was opened in 1937, but was later vandalized. The last of the stops offers a beautiful view of Grand Valley in which Grand Junction is located and other interesting views of the geology and landforms of the area. The entire hike of approximately 0.75 miles (1.2 kilometers) takes about 30 to 45 minutes to complete.

Before leaving the immediate vicinity of Grand Junction, present day dinosaur hunters should visit Dinosaur Valley located in Grand Junction. This museum is unlike many others because along with the usual articulated dinosaur skeletons and fossils from around the area, Dinosaur Valley features animated scale model dinosaur robots (Figure 80) which greet visitors with movements and bellows. These robotic dinosaurs are all scale models of the mighty reptiles that inhabited the Grand Junction area over 140-million years ago as the Morrison Formation was being deposited. Unlike many other museums, the exhibits at Dinosaur Valley are all about the local paleontology. Besides displays, a public paleontological preparation laboratory is enjoyed by visitors (Figure 81). Dinosaur Valley is open daily and admission is charged.

Another one of the old Riggs' quarries is easily accessible from Interstate 70 (Figure 79). Travelers along the interstate may take the Fruita exit west of Grand Junction and head south on Highway 340 about 1 mile (1.67 kilometers) to the hill which will be on the east or left side of the highway. A turnoff leads to a parking area with ample spaces for leaving one's car or recreational vehicle while hiking on the trail. Dinosaur Hill may also be reached from Riggs Hill by taking Highway 340, or South Broadway, west. The trailhead to Dinosaur Hill is marked by a large boulder which long ago broke away from the Morrison Formation and slid downhill

Figure 80. Half-size scale-model robotic dinosaurs, including this *Stegosaurus* made by Dinamation International, move and howl at Dinosaur Valley, part of the Museum of Western Colorado in Grand Junction.

(Figure 82). This boulder contains the mold, or impression, of a femur (thigh bone) of a sauropod. Well into the middle 1900s the bone remained in the rock, but vandals eventually removed the bone leaving only the mold. A mile long (1.67 kilometers) trail with ten stops acquaints tourists with information about the geology of the Morrison Formation and the site where Riggs and his crew had to use dynamite to free the fossilized bones of *Apatosaurus* (*Brontosaurus*) from the hard rocks of the Morrison. Again check the box at the trailhead sign for copies of the guide to the numbered stops. This is the site where part of the tail of *Apatosaurus* may still be in the hillside. A plaque commemorates the old quarry site. Hikers should allow about 1 hour of walking to take in the sights of the trail.

Figure 81. Dinosaur Valley in Grand Junction features a public fossil preparation laboratory where visitors can watch technicians preparing dinosaur fossils for display. Pictured here is Harold Bollan, a retired teacher and avid dinosaur collector.

Figure 82. A mile-long (1.67 kilometer) interpretive trail at Dinosaur Hill south of Fruita starts out with a boulder from the Morrison that has the mold of impression of a femur (thigh bone) of a large sauropod.

Hikers should remember that all of these trails discussed are on protected public lands and it is unlawful for visitors to take anything from these sites. As the saying goes, take only pictures and leave only footprints.

Another bit of landscape often holds travelers for one more day in this region. West of Grand Junction an area of rugged beauty awaits the visitor at Colorado National Monument which lies on the northeast side of the Uncompahgre Plateau (Figure 79). This plateau is a geologic structure which has been uplifted several times in the past and remains high today. Visitors are greeted with sheer cliffs whose weathered and stained sandstone faces record the presence of Colorado's Early Mesozoic deserts. The road which winds

West of Grand Junction almost at the Utah border dinosaur enthusiasts can visit a present day research site at Rabbit Valley (Figure 78). From Interstate 70, travelers should take the well marked exit at milepost 2 for Rabbit Valley. This site is immediately north of the interstate and again ample parking for cars or recreational vehicles is available. Rabbit Valley is another joint venture between the Museum of Western Colorado and the BLM. The Mygatt-Moore Dinosaur Quarry (see Figure 69 in Chapter 8) is located to the northwest of the trailhead of the Trail Through Time. This interpretive trail winds over the topography of the Morrison Formation for 1.5 miles (2.5 kilometer) and is moderately strenuous (Figure 83). Stops along the trail

include some of the sandstone lenses which were deposited by ancient rivers and contain dinosaur bones in the now well lithified sandstone. Other signposts acquaint visitors with the natural history and rugged beauty of this desert environment (Figure 84). Like other trails in this area, a pamphlet is available at the trailhead.

Figure 83. Hikers start out on the Trail Through Time at the Rabbit Valley Research Area, west of Grand Junction near the Utah Border.

its way through these massive cliffs to the top of the plateau offers many breathtaking views of the vast Grand Valley where Grand Junction lies. Views from the top are equally inspiring with more panoramas of Grand Valley and canyons which have cut deeply into the Uncompahgre Plateau. An admission fee is charged at the monument.

To the north of Colorado National Monument about 120 miles (194 kilometers), more beautiful scenery and dinosaurs await travelers at Dinosaur National Monument. The monument straddles the Colorado-Utah border in northwest Colorado (Figure 76) and is located north of the town of Dinosaur, Colorado along U.S. Highway 40. This national treasure covers land in Colorado and Utah and has been a popular stop throughout the years. Both the natural beauty and dinosaur fossils make Dinosaur National Monument a fantastic stop. Visitors wishing to reach the monument from the Grand Junction area, should take Colorado Highway 139 north to the town of Rangely. Just east of Rangely is the intersection of Highway 139 with State Highway 64. Take Highway 64 west to the town of Dinosaur, Colorado where Highway 64 meets U.S. Highway 40. This scenic drive offers many impressive views of rocks ranging in age from Jurassic through Tertiary. Whether coming from the south around Grand Junction or from the east along U.S. 40, visitors may want to take a short detour through the

Figure 84. This view looks south from a point on the Rabbit Valley Trail Through Time. In the distance are the La Sal Mountains and in the middle and foreground are the Mesozoic rocks on the northwest flank of the Uncompahgre Plateau.

town of Dinosaur where streets are named for dinosaurs and street signs feature renditions of the various popular dinosaurs. Dinosaur National Monument may also be reached from the west on U.S. 40.

Some of Dinosaur National Monument's scenic splendor may be viewed by heading east on U.S. 40 from the town of Dinosaur. Just east of town, on the north side of Highway 40, is a clearly marked turnoff for a visitor's center on the Colorado side of the Monument. Explorers can become familiar with the geology, natural history, and scenery of the Monument which is a large anticlinal, or upward-folded structure. This large upward bend in the earth's surface has brought rocks of the Jurassic Morrison Formation and older rocks to the surface. Subsequent erosion by rivers has created deep and beau-

tiful canyons on this structure. This anticline was formed during the mountain building episode that is responsible for the present day Rocky Mountains

After viewing some of the scenery, explorers will want to return to U.S. 40 and head west to the town of Jensen, Utah which lies 18 miles (30 kilometers) west of the Colorado-Utah border. In Jensen take the clearly marked Utah Highway 149 north 6 miles (16 kilometers) to visit the quarry. There is ample parking available at the dinosaur quarry and shuttle buses transport people from the parking lots to the large building which protects the quarry face and holds many new and refurbished exhibits (refer to Figures 13 and 14 in Chapter 2). The building which covers the quarry was first opened to the public in 1958. Exhibits were expanded and renovated during the late 1980s and reflect new interpretations about the life-style and behavior of the dinosaurs. An admission fee is charged at the quarry.

Visiting any or all of Colorado's many dinosaur attractions can be a rewarding educational and enjoyable experience for children and adults. For years dinosaurs have been a popular topic for children. Teachers are now recognizing that the innate fascination that children have for dinosaurs may be used to develop an appreciation and love for science. Also many adults can expand their horizons with the many indoor and outdoor dinosaur attractions that the state of Colorado has to offer. Colorado's many attractions will continue to provide hours of enjoyment in the years to come.

DINO SOURCES

Denver Museum of Natural History
2001 Colorado Blvd.
Denver, CO 80205
(303) 322-7009
Earth Sciences Dept. (303) 370-6473
Education Dept. (303) 370-6371

Dinosaur Hill
1.5 mile south of Fruita on
Highway 340
c/o Dinosaur Valley
(303) 241-9210

Dinosaur National Monument
P. O. Box 210
Dinosaur, CO 81610
(303) 374-2216

Dinosaur Valley
4th and Main
Grand Junction, CO 81502-5020
(303) 243-3466

Friends of Dinosaur Ridge
c/o Morrison Natural History Museum
P. O. Box 564
Morrison, CO 80465
(303) 697-1873

Garden Park Fossil Area
Eight miles north of Canon City on
County Highway 9
(719) 275-2331

Picket Wire Canyonlands
c/o Comanche National Grassland
P. O. Box 817
La Junta, CO 81050
(719) 384-2181

Rabbit Valley Quarry
30 miles west of Grand Junction,
Rabbit Valley Exit on I-70
(303) 241-9210

Riggs Hill
Highway 340 west from Grand Junction to South Broadway and Meadows Way
c/o Dinosaur Valley
(303) 241-9210

University of Colorado at Boulder Museum
Henderson Bldg.
15th and Broadway
Campus Box 218
Boulder, CO 80302
(303) 492-6892
Geology Dept. (303) 492-8142

SELECTED REFERENCES AND FURTHER READING

People interested in obtaining more information about dinosaurs have the rather unique problem of sorting through the available literature. Unfortunately with the surge in dinosaur research of the past few years much of the material about dinosaurs is out of date or erroneous. Dinosaur enthusiasts may want to check with their local library, bookstore or perhaps the gift shops at any of Colorado's dinosaur attractions for the following titles which reflect current ideas about dinosaurs. This list is extremely abbreviated, but contains titles which the authors of this book either consult frequently or feel are scientifically accurate in their presentation of the topic.

Children will enjoy either being read to or can read about dinosaurs in:

A Dictionary of Dinosaurs, 101 from A to Z by Rupert Matthews, 1988, published by Derrydale Books, 48 pages, ages 7–11.

The Big Book of Dinosaurs by Dougal Dixon, 1989, published by Derrydale Books, 128 pages, ages 7–11.

Dinosaur books by Janet Riehecky, 1988. This author has produced a number of books about dinosaurs for young readers that cover a specific dinosaur in each of her nine titles. Titles currently include: *Allosaurus, Apatosaurus, Anatosaurus, Brachiosaurus, Iguanodon, Maiasaura, Stegosaurus, Triceratops* and *Tyrannosaurus rex*, published by Children's Press, each book 32 pages, ages 4–9.

Adults will no doubt enjoy the following publications:

The Dinosaur Heresies by Dr. Robert Bakker, 1986, published by William Morrow and Co., Inc. Dr. Bakker uses his own illustrations and unique readable style of writing to argue against some of the theories about dinosaurs that many academicians have held sacred for years.

On the Trail of the Dinosaurs by Michael Benton, 1989, published by Crescent Books, 144 pages. Dr. Benton discusses the worldwide occurrence of dinosaurs as well as the many different types of theses animals. This book is very well illustrated with many full color photographs and illustrations

A New Look at Dinosaurs by Dr. Alan Charig, 1983, published by Facts On File, Inc., 160 pages. This is a great and affordable book for anyone interested in a more detailed explanation of the evolutionary status of the dinosaurs as well as the history of dinosaur research.

An Illustrated Encyclopedia of Dinosaurs by Dr. David Norman, 1985, published by Crescent Books, 208 pages. This is probably the most definitive book written for the interested layman. It is often used in college-level survey courses about dinosaurs. It contains many illustrations including full-color restorations of dinosaurs.

Digging Dinosaurs by John R. Horner, 1988, published by Workman Publishing Company, 210 pages. This book gives readers a firsthand look at exploring for dinosaurs in the field and then collecting the fossils. It is based upon Horner's own experience of collecting dinosaurs in Montana. An excellent account of how today's dinosaur researcher pieces together the clues that can be woven into a detailed account of how dinosaurs lived.

Dinosaurs by Dr. David Norman, 1987, published by Crescent Books, 48 pages, an 11-inch x 17-inch poster book. Subsequent to his encyclopedia about dinosaurs, Dr. Norman produced this large-format book which features full-color illustrations by noted dinosaur artist John Sibbick. An excellent reference for teachers who want to show their classes scientifically accurate color illustrations of dinosaurs in action.

Dinosaurs of North America by Dr. Dale Russell, 1989, published by NorthWord Press, 240 pages. Dr. Russell discusses what dinosaurs have been discovered in North America, where the fossils have been found and much about the behavior of these animals in this large-format and colorfully illustrated book.

Dinosaur Tour Book by William Lee Stokes, 1988, published by Starstone Publishing Company, 64 pages. Dr. Stokes, a retired professor of geology, has compiled a listing of most of the dinosaur attractions in the western United States, southern Canada and northwestern Mexico. The many listings are compiled state by state in a readable style.

The Great Dinosaur Hunters by Edwin Colbert, 1984, published by Dover Publication, Inc., 283 pages. This book is the definitive text for people wanting to know more about the famous dinosaur collectors and the sites where these discoveries were made. This enjoy book is a must for anyone interested in a good historical perspective of worldwide dinosaur research.

Pathway to the Dinosaurs, Map No. 1, Colorado, Wyoming and Utah,1987, published by Dino Productions. This geologic highway map (a 24-inch x 36-inch travel/wall map) highlights rocks from the Mesozoic Era (Age of Reptiles) in Colorado, Wyoming and Utah. An informative text that discusses the major discoveries in these three states and where they can be seen. This map is for sale at either the Colorado Geological Survey or from Dino Productions, P. O. Box 3004, Englewood, Colorado 80155-3004.

INDEX

A

aetosaur 25, 26, 36

Age of Invertebrates 15

Age of Mammals 15, 19, 51

Age of Reptiles 2, 15, 18, 72

Albertosaurus 51

allosaurid 26, 58

Allosaurus 4, 6, 39, 43, 57–59, 61, 65, 71

American Museum 11

amphibian 41, 42, 56

ankylosaurid 30, 31, 51, 57

Apatosaurus 7, 10, 28, 57–59, 67, 71

Apatosaurus excelsus 9

Apatosaurus louisae 11

Archibald, Dr. David 22, 59

B

Bakker, Dr. Robert 61, 65, 71

Barosaurus 59

basin 18

bentonite 42, 56

bipedal 25, 26, 29–31, 36, 41, 58

bird 23, 24, 29, 30, 32, 41, 47, 51, 58

bison 6, 8, 50

body fossil 27, 35, 43, 49

Book Cliffs 22

brachiosaurid 10, 28, 29, 41

Brachiosaurus 28, 40, 41, 57, 58, 71

Brachiosaurus altithorax 8, 9, 40, 66

Bradbury, Samuel M. 9

Brigham Young University (BYU) 10, 58

Bureau of Land Management (BLM) 6, 55, 57, 60, 65, 66, 68

C

California State University 55, 56

Camarasaurus 4, 10, 28, 57–59

Cambrian 15

Camptosaurus 58, 59

Canon City, Colorado 1, 3–5, 41, 48, 60, 63, 65, 70

Carnegie, Andrew 11

Carnegie, Louise 11

Carnegie Museum of Natural History 4, 6, 10, 11, 12

carnivore, carnivorous 4, 8, 21, 24, 25, 27–29, 38, 39, 41–43, 45, 47, 50, 51, 56, 59

carnosaur 29, 58

Cenozoic 15, 19, 64

ceratopsian 9, 30, 31, 50, 61

Ceratosaurus 39, 43, 56, 58, 59

Chinle Formation 20, 34

Cleveland Museum of Natural History 4, 6, 60

coal 21, 22, 46, 48, 49

coal swamp 22, 48–50

Coelophysis 35, 36

coelurosaur 29, 58

coelurosaurid 29, 41, 58

Coelurus 58

Colorado National Monument 4, 68, 69

Colorado School of Mines 22, 56, 57

columnar section 19

Como Bluff 7

continental drift 35, 38

Cope, Edward Drinker 4–7, 27, 32, 60, 63, 65

Craig, Colorado 4, 21, 48, 59

Cretaceous 4, 8, 18, 20–22, 26, 29–31, 34, 40, 41, 43, 45–54, 58–61, 64

crocodile 5, 25, 36, 39, 41

cross section 17, 61

Cross, Whitman 8

crossbeds 34

cycad 28, 29, 31, 39

D

Dakota Group 20–22, 26, 60, 61, 64

Dakota Hogback 1, 7, 60

Deinonychus 29

Delta, Colorado 4, 9, 10, 37, 40, 42, 56, 58

Delta County Museum 4

Denver Basin 53, 54

Denver Beds 8

Denver, Colorado 3, 4, 7, 8, 21, 26, 29, 38, 47, 50, 52, 53

Denver Formation 20, 22, 29, 50, 53, 54

Denver Museum of Natural History 4, 6, 8, 48, 60, 62, 64, 65, 70

DeWeese, Dallas 5, 6

Dinamation International 57, 67

Dinosaur, Colorado 4, 11, 69, 70

Dinosaur Hill 10, 67, 68, 70

Dinosaur National Monument 4, 6, 10–12, 26, 28, 55, 59, 65, 69, 70

Dinosaur Ridge 1, 7, 8, 12, 51, 60, 61, 63, 64

Dinosaur Trackers Research Group 8

Dinosaur Valley 4, 56, 57, 66, 67, 70

dinosauria 23

diplodocid 10, 28, 29, 39, 40

Diplodocus 5, 6, 11, 28, 58, 59, 65

Douglass, Earl 11, 12, 28

dromeosaur 58

Dry Mesa Quarry 10, 37, 40, 41, 58

Dryosaurus 58, 59

E

Earth Science Museum 58

Echinodon 28, 41, 56

Edmontosaurus 65

egg 2, 6, 20, 23, 29, 31, 38, 42, 58, 60

Epanterias 39, 61

Euoplocephalus 31

extinction 22, 31, 43, 45, 51, 53, 54, 58

F

femur 11, 67, 68

fern 53, 54

Field Columbian Museum 9

Field Museum of Natural History 4, 9, 10

fish 5, 42, 56, 57

footprint 7, 8, 20, 21, 26, 27, 34–36, 38, 43, 46–49, 61

Fort Collins, Colorado 61

fossilization 13, 14, 49

Friends of Dinosaur Ridge 8, 61, 70, inside back cover

Fruita, Colorado 10, 56, 67, 68, 70

Fruita Paleontological Area 17, 41, 55–57

G

Garden Park, Colorado 1, 4–7, 12, 41, 60, 65, 70

Garden Park Paleontological Society 6, 60, 65

geologic column 19

geologic time scale 14

Golden, Colorado 1, 6, 7, 22, 54, 57, 63

Goodrich, George 11

Grand Junction, Colorado 3, 4, 8, 9, 12, 17, 20, 22, 27, 35, 36, 40–42, 47, 55–59, 63, 66–70

gymnosperm 39, 42

H

hadrosaur 47–51, 59

Haplocanthosaurus 6

Hayden, Dr. Ferdinand V. 4

Hayden Territorial Surveys 11

herbivore, herbivorous 7–11, 21, 24, 25, 27–32, 36, 38–42, 47, 48, 51, 58

Holland, Dr. William J. 11

horned dinosaur 8, 9, 50

Horner, Jack 49, 72

I

iguanodontid 26, 47, 58, 61

iridium 52, 53

igneous rocks 15

J

Jensen, Utah 59, 69

Jones, Ed and Vivian 10